CONTENTS

INTRODUCTION

Hello! In picking up this book, you have chosen to leap into the fantastic world of sustainable living and, for that, Mother Nature would like to say "thank you". Hopefully, this lovely little book will provide you with some new ideas about how you can reduce your carbon footprint and live a more eco-conscious life.

As I'm sure you are aware, our earth is beautiful but our ecosystem is fragile. If we all keep living the fast-paced, high-carbon-footprint, disposable lifestyles we've come to know and love, then we're sure to irreparably shorten the time we've got on our wonderful planet. However, it isn't *entirely* too-little-too-late! Every single one of us could make a change to protect our home, so why not use a few of these hacks to help you along the way?

PLANET-FRIENDLY HACKS

Simple Tips and Budget-Friendly
Advice for Sustainable Living

ELIZABETH AJAO

An Hachette UK Company
www.hachette.co.uk

Summersdale Publishers Ltd
Part of Octopus Publishing Group Limited
Carmelite House
50 Victoria Embankment
LONDON
EC4Y 0DZ
UK

www.summersdale.com

Printed and bound in Poland

ISBN: 978-1-80007-402-6

Substantial discounts on bulk quantities of Summersdale books are available to corporations, professional associations and other organizations. For details contact general enquiries: telephone: +44 (0) 1243 771107 or email: enquiries@summersdale.com.

Neither the author nor the publisher can be held responsible for any loss, damage or injury – be it health, financial or otherwise – arising out of the use, or misuse, of the suggestions made herein.

In this book, you'll find seven chapters featuring hacks, recipes and handy craft ideas to help you live with a more planet-friendly mindset.

Avoid purchasing new things for these DIYs; the most planet-friendly way to do them is to reuse what you've already got lying around. It's also worth finding alternatives if you don't have all the right equipment. Go on, get creative!

From eco-friendly cleaning products to sustainable self-care solutions, from creating capsule wardrobes to adopting greener habits on your travels, there's something in here for everyone wanting to live a more planet-friendly life.

THE LOW-DOWN
on Climate Change

The concentration of carbon dioxide in the air was recorded as 419 ppm (parts per million) in 2021 – the highest figure it's been for over 3 million years.

Humans are responsible for releasing 26.4 gigatonnes (that's the weight of approximately 160 million blue whales!) of carbon dioxide into the atmosphere every year.

Sea levels are rising at a rate of 3.6 mm per year, and by the year 2100, they could have risen another 1.1 m. That would mean 2 billion people (approx. one fifth of the population) would lose their homes and be forced to move further inland.

Landfills don't just take up space, they also produce a *lot* of gas; which is mostly carbon dioxide and methane.

If the population keeps growing at its current rate, the annual worldwide waste is likely to grow to 3.4 billion tonnes by 2050. Given that the United Kingdom is nearly out of landfill space, this is very concerning.

Climate change massively impacts the weather, and, whether that comes in the form of freak storms or severe droughts, it's having a huge effect on those in developing countries who are forced to flee their homes. By 2050, 200 million people could be displaced due to climate change.

By considering the world's needs as well as our own, we can live cleaner, happier lives.

CLEANING HACKS

How many eco-unfriendly products feature in your cleaning routine? We're so used to harsh chemicals and disposable dishcloths that we often forget how damaging they are to the planet. Want to ditch those harmful habits and swap your landfill-bound wipes for some DIY reusable ones? Well, read on and learn...

DODGY DRAINS?

Is the stench of your drain getting you down? Then, this hack for cleaning drains without expensive and toxic chemicals is perfect for you.

Try pouring 125 g (4½ oz) baking soda down the drain, followed by a mixture of 250 ml (8½ fl oz) white vinegar and the juice of half a lemon. Leave it for 5 minutes, then pour approximately 3.5 litres (118 fl oz) hot water down the drain to clear the mix away. Now it should smell citrusy fresh!

Sparkling-clean drain

No more weird smell

DIY DISHWASHER TABLETS

Did you know that most dishwasher tablets are made with toxins, phosphates and plastic, which are wrecking our waterways and killing our marvellous marine life? Here's a simple hack to wash your dishes without harming our fish.

Your one-way ticket to beautiful, clean dishes

METHOD:

1   Mix together 120 g (4 oz) washing soda (there are tips on how to make this on page 14), 240 g (8 oz) baking soda, 120 g (4 oz) Epsom salts, 120 g (4 oz) lemon juice and around 40 drops of your choice of essential oil. Your mixture should feel damp, so add a few more tablespoons of lemon juice (one at a time!) if it's too crumbly.

2   Firmly press your mixture into an ice tray (make each "tablet" no more than 2 cm (⅘ in.) thick if your dishwasher has a tablet compartment).

3   Leave them to dry out for around 24 hours.

4   Once hardened, carefully remove them from the tray and store in an airtight container.

5   Just pop one tablet into your dishwasher as usual and let it work its magic.

HOMEMADE
WORKTOP WIPES

When life gives you lemons, make cleaning wipes! Here's a hack for minimizing your kitchen waste and making a super-citrusy, non-toxic, all-purpose cleaner. You'll need some lemons, distilled vinegar, old T-shirts, fresh mint, tea tree oil and a large jar. It's best not to use these on marble, granite or wood surfaces, just in case they're damaged by the acidity.

Citrusy fresh!

METHOD:

1   Squeeze the juice out of several lemons (why not set this aside to make some homemade lemonade?), put the rinds in a large jar and cover them with distilled vinegar. Add some fresh mint and tea tree oil, as these oils have antiseptic qualities.

2   Seal the jar and store it away from sunlight for at least a week – the longer you leave it the stronger the scent will be.

3   Once ready, strain the mixture into a bowl to remove any solid pulp. Do this as many times as needed; after all, you don't want mint leaves ingrained into your kitchen counters. Rinse the jar and set aside for later. TIP: If the scent is too overpowering, dilute the fluid with water – this will also make it go further!

4   Cut up some old T-shirts into 20×20-cm (8×8-in.) squares. Fold them in half and roll into coils. One by one, stuff these into the jar.

5   Pour your liquid into the jar, ensuring your wipes are fully saturated.

6   Your wipes are ready! Use to wipe down surfaces and keep them sparkling clean!

Top Tips:

Cleaning with baking soda

Bins stink. It's a fact. However, baking soda is great at removing yucky smells. Sprinkle some in the bottom of your bin liner or bin and it'll neutralize any nasty odours.

Instead of wasting money and plastic by purchasing chemical-based sofa cleaners, sprinkle a layer of baking soda over the cushions and leave it for 20 minutes before hoovering it off for a fresh-smelling sofa.

Make your own washing soda by pouring baking soda into a baking tray and putting it in the oven at 200°C (400°F) for 45 minutes – this evaporates the water content, leaving sodium carbonate (Na_2CO_3) or, as we know it, washing soda. Remember to let it cool before use and pop it in an airtight container to store it.

Soap-scummy sink? Coat the affected area with baking soda, scrub with a sponge and then spritz with three squirts of hydrogen peroxide. Let it sit for a few minutes then rinse away – clean as a... new sink?

TOP TIPS:

Cleaning with fabrics

Got a flat mop but don't want to keep buying disposable covers? Use a stray, holey, fluffy sock. Stretch it over the base of your mop and clean away.

Even better than purchasing microfibre cloths, for heavy-duty cleaning you can reuse cotton, thick flannel or other lint-free clothing you no longer wear. Thin materials, such as chiffon and linen, are great for dusting, polishing furniture and buffing metal.

If you want to live clutter-free *and* waste-free, why not swap kitchen roll for microfibre cloths? Just add water – some are even antibacterial too.

DIY KITCHEN SCRUBBERS

Keep the kitchen squeaky clean without the need for disposable sponges with this crafty idea. Don't get rid of your old sponges just yet, though, as they'll come in handy on page 71!

PER SCRUBBER, YOU WILL NEED:

- One 13×18-cm (5×7-in.) 100 per cent cotton rectangle

- Four 13×18-cm (5×7-in.) flannel rectangles (use more if you'd prefer thicker scrubbers)

- One 13×18-cm (5×7-in.) rectangle of muslin, waffle or burlap

- Pins, a needle and thread

- Scissors or a rotary cutter

- Sewing machine (optional)

Not your average scrubber

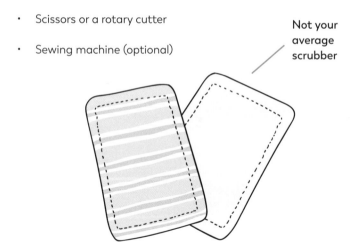

METHOD:

1 Place the flannel fabric on your workspace. Lay the muslin, waffle or burlap on top, then put the cotton on top of that. Pin these layers together.

2 Leaving a 1-cm (⅜-in.) seam allowance around the edge, stitch around the perimeter of the fabric, leaving a 5-cm (2-in.) gap on one of the longer sides.

3 Trim down your seam allowance by 0.5 cm (⅛ in.) (this will make it less bulky later). When you get to each corner, snip at a 45-degree angle.

4 Using your 5-cm (2-in.) gap, turn the whole thing inside out. You should have one cotton side and a scrubbing side, and all your flannel layers should be hidden inside.

5 Stitch around the edge of your pad, leaving a 1-cm (⅜-in.) seam allowance. NOTE: This might be tricky as it'll be thick!

6 *Et voila!* Your very own washable, reusable, recycled, compostable washing-up scrubber.

NO MORE
MUCKY MICROWAVES

Microwaves are an absolute nightmare to clean. Porridge oats cemented to the ceiling, last night's bolognaise spattered on the walls and an inexplicable noodle shrivelled up in the corner from goodness knows when. Rather than use a strong chemical cleaner, here's a greener way to clean up the mess that's just as effective.

Take one slice of lemon and pop it in a microwave-safe bowl filled halfway with water. Put it in the microwave and blast for around a minute or until the water is boiled. Leave the door closed for a couple of minutes before you start cleaning it – and thanks to the mini steam room you've created, the stains should wipe away with ease!

Dirty microwave

Lemon, ready to
work its magic

CRYSTAL-CLEAR WINDOWS

Smudgy windows are no joke – how are you supposed to know which thrifted jacket to wear if you can't see what the weather's like? This simple two-ingredient hack will keep your windows perfectly pristine.

Using a bottle of white vinegar, spritz your dirty windows all over. Scrunch up an old newspaper and, using it like you would a cloth, scrub your windows to your heart's content. Replace the newspaper when it starts to get soggy, then you're done.

Sparkling, or what?

TOP TIPS:
Cleaning with tea

Are streaky glass and stainless steel making your glossy appliances an eyesore? Simply make a cup of black tea with a teabag you've already used (skip the milk) and leave it to cool down. Dip a cloth (or the soft side of your homemade scrubber – see page 16) into the tea and give your glass or metal a good clean with it. It might look streaky to start with, but it'll dry streak-free!

Sick of wasting chemicals and energy scrubbing greasy dishes and utensils? Try filling a washing-up bowl with warm water as you usually would, but place two or three used teabags into the water with the dirty dishes, and leave to soak for 5 minutes. The tannins will reduce the grease, making the washing-up less of a chore!

Here's a simple tip to keep your toilet clean. Throw a used teabag into the toilet and leave it to soak overnight. In the morning, give it a scrub and you'll have a sparkling clean toilet bowl.

Top Tips:
Cleaning with lemon juice

If your wooden chopping board is looking a bit worse for wear, don't bin it – fix it. Coat the board in cooking salt and the juice of half a lemon, and give the surface a little scrub (with a sponge or your homemade scrubber – see page 16). Let it sit for 5 minutes then clean it off with a damp sponge. Fresh as a daisy!

Hard water ruining the chrome in your bathroom? Cut a lemon in half and simply rub it all over your taps and handles. Tie an old plastic shopping bag around the lemon-soaked chrome and leave it for a few hours. Simply wipe with a clean cloth and the citric acid should have removed all of the limescale.

Plastic food containers always end up stained a curry-bolognaise orange, but by rubbing lemon juice all over the surface and leaving it for 15 minutes before rinsing off, you can give your Tupperware new life!

SUSTAINABLE SWAPS:
The laundry edition

Try these simple swaps to make your laundry routine more eco-friendly:

- To whiten whites, swap chlorine/bleach-based stain remover for lemon juice or white vinegar – but double-check whether your fabric takes well to acidity first.

- It's better to skip tumble-drying entirely, but if you *must* tumble-dry something and want to make your laundry feel soft, use wool dryer balls instead of plastic-based dryer sheets.

- Use powder detergents, which come in cardboard packaging, instead of bottled liquid detergents.

- Although we tend to associate beautifully scented detergents with cleanliness, unscented products are less damaging to the planet because they contain fewer chemicals.

DIY LAUNDRY DETERGENT

Not only are most shop-bought detergents bad for the planet, they're not great for your skin, either. Why not try making your own?

Mix 65 g (2¼ oz) Epsom salts, 65 g (2¼ oz) baking soda, 190 g (6½ oz) washing soda, 30 g (1 oz) sea salt and 20–25 drops of essential oils – eucalyptus, grapefruit, lemon, rose or lavender are great scents for lovely smelling laundry. Store in an airtight jar and when you need it use 1–2 tbsp per load.

A spoonful of your finest planet-friendly detergent

DETERGENT

CLEAN THAT CARPET

Carpets are soft, squishy and *so* cosy on the feet, but they stain easily. However, all is not lost, because with this simple, chemical-free hack you can save your carpet *and* the planet.

Try spritzing the stain with white vinegar, cover it with an old white T-shirt, then, using the steam setting on your iron, iron over the top of the T-shirt. TIP: Make sure you keep moving your iron around so that you don't burn or singe the carpet underneath. The stain should lift away – ta-da!

Weird stains, begone!

RUST BUSTER

Rust isn't pretty. It creeps into all sorts of things, such as once-pristine garden furniture, bicycles and even cars. You might think the only solution is to throw the item out and hope the local scrap metal collector will find a use for it. However, it's easier than you think to remove rust from metal. All you need is recyclable aluminium foil, white vinegar and a little elbow grease.

Simply dip the foil in the vinegar, then gently scrub the affected area before wiping it clean with a smooth cloth. Remember to recycle the foil!

Rust-busting vinegar

Humble aluminium foil

WHITE VINEGAR

TOP TIPS:

Cleaning with coconut and olive oil

If your extractor fan is coated in a dusty, sticky, oily film, you can easily loosen the film with coconut or olive oil, then gently wipe it away using a damp cloth with soap.

To remove sticky patches from jars, bottles and crockery, peel off as much of the label as you can, mix baking soda and coconut oil together in equal parts, apply the solution and leave it for a few minutes before wiping clean.

TOP TIPS:

Cleaning with miscellaneous items

Clean food-encrusted dishes and cast-iron pots and pans by putting a broken eggshell in the pan, then scrubbing it around with a soap-covered sponge.

Use a pumice stone to remove tough hard water stains from the toilet, sink or even bath. TIP: Don't scrub too hard in case you scratch the surface!

After use, keep any old antibacterial/cleaning spray bottles for homemade cleaning spray so you don't increase your carbon footprint by purchasing new ones.

SUSTAINABLE TOILET SCRUB

Bleach is dreadful for our health *and* our planet, and we don't need it for effective cleaning anyway. Give this easy-peasy bleach-free toilet-cleaning hack a go instead.

Next time you're cleaning your toilet, try mixing 30 g (1 oz) baking soda with 230 ml (7⅘ fl oz) white vinegar. Pour it into the toilet bowl, leave for a few minutes and scrub it off before flushing!

The throne, finally restored to a sparkling finish

KITCHEN HACKS

The kitchen is a real hub for waste, from our plastic-packaged food to energy-sapping appliances. Even though the kitchen might seem like the least environmentally friendly room in the house, there are plenty of hacks to keep your carbon footprint down.

MAKE YOUR OWN BEESWAX FOOD WRAP

Beeswax food wraps are an amazing, relatively new alternative to cling film, which emits dioxin (a very toxic chemical) when sent to landfill. But do not fear, for beeswax wrap is here to keep your food fresh for longer, and, while it's fairly pricey to buy, it's easy-peasy-lemon-bee-zy to make!

YOU WILL NEED:

- Beeswax pellets
- Clean 100 per cent cotton fabric cut into 20×20-cm (8×8-in.) squares
- Scissors
- Metal bulldog clips
- Large paintbrush
- Baking paper
- Large, lipped baking tray
- Tongs
- 1 hanger (with clips) per fabric square

Care tip: Scrunch the beeswax wrap for a minute or two in your hands before each use to melt the wax a little and make it malleable. Wash the wraps in cold water with mild soap then hang to dry. Remember not to use them around anything that might melt the wax and don't use on raw meat.

METHOD:

1   Preheat your oven to 140°C (275°F) and line your baking tray with baking paper.

2   Place your fabric on top – if it's patterned, keep the patterned side facing down.

3   Spread the beeswax pellets over the fabric then cover with another layer of baking paper – use metal bulldog clips to keep the baking paper attached to your fabric.

4   Pop in the oven for 5 minutes, or until the wax pellets have melted.

5   Spread the melted wax over the fabric using your dry paintbrush. Only one side needs to be wax-coated, the other can be left bare so it doesn't make your picnic box or cupboard all waxy. TIP: Wipe off excess wax and run the brush under hot water immediately after to ensure it isn't ruined.

6   Carefully picking up your fabric with tongs (avoid touching any wax, as it will be hot), waft it in the air for a few seconds to cool. Then, clip it onto your hanger and wait for it to dry.

7   Bish-bash-bosh, you've got your very own beeswax wraps!

FABULOUS FENNEL AND SPINACH TART

After you've made this delicious meal, place the base of your fennel bulb in a glass filled with 250 ml (8½ fl oz) water and put it on the windowsill. Once the roots start to grow, plant it in the garden and after 2–3 months you'll have a big enough fennel to make another tasty tart!

YOU WILL NEED:

- 60 g (2 oz) unsalted butter (or dairy-free equivalent)
- 3 red onions, sliced
- 300 g (10½ oz) frozen spinach (thawed and strained)
- 1 tbsp olive oil
- 2 fennel bulbs, thinly sliced horizontally and stalks halved lengthways (remember to keep the core for planting)
- ½ tsp ground cumin
- ½ tsp fennel seeds, crushed
- 120 g (4 oz) sugar
- 375 g (13 oz) sheet puff pastry
- A splash of milk (or dairy-free equivalent)
- 2 tsp olive oil
- Juice of half a lemon
- Handful of grated cheddar (or dairy-free equivalent)

METHOD:

1   Preheat the oven to 180°C (350°F) and grease an ovenproof dish.

2   Melt your butter in a large frying pan over a medium heat, stir in the onion and fennel bulbs then cook, stirring continuously, for 5–10 minutes or until they start to colour.

3   Meanwhile, heat your olive oil in a separate pan over a medium heat. Once hot, add your spinach and let it cook until it's wilted. Drain and squeeze it to get rid of excess water, and pat dry with a paper towel if needed.

4   Add the cumin, fennel seeds and sugar to your onion and fennel mix, and cook for 10 minutes or until caramelized. Stir in the spinach, then pour the mixture into your dish.

5   On a flat surface, cut a piece of pastry the shape and size of your dish. Place it over the top of your fennel mixture, press the edges with the prongs of a fork to seal and brush with a little milk to make it shiny. Bake for 15 minutes.

6   Meanwhile, mix the oil, lemon juice and fennel stalks in a bowl.

7   When the tart is ready, remove it from the oven and drizzle your dressing over the top. Coat in cheese and enjoy!

MAKE YOUR OWN REUSABLE TEABAGS

Put the kettle on – it's teatime! But when you're done with the bag, where does it go? Several big-brand tea companies use polypropylene to seal their teabags, so popping them in the compost bin isn't as eco-friendly as you might think. Why not try making your very own reusable teabags? They're great for personal use and make lovely eco-friendly gifts too!

YOU WILL NEED:

- Thin 100 per cent cotton fabric, cut into 8×12-cm (3×5-in.) rectangles (one per bag)

- 100 per cent cotton twine or string, cut into 35-cm (14-in.) lengths (one per bag)

- Needle and cotton thread, or a sewing machine

- Scissors

- Sewing pins

- Iron and ironing board

Ready for your favourite tea

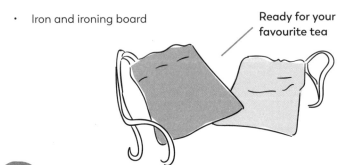

METHOD:

1   Wash, dry and iron your fabric, then fold the longer side in by 0.5 cm (⅛ in.). Do this again on the same side to hide the raw edge. Stitch along the fold.

2   Tie your twine or string around your needle, then thread it through the fabric tunnel you've created.

3   Turn the fabric over so that your folded side is facing down, then fold the fabric in half as though it's a Christmas card.

4   Pin in place, then stitch around the raw edges, about 0.5 cm (⅛ in.) in from the edge, making sure you don't sew right up to the string. You should now have a little pouch.

5   Turn the whole thing inside out – all of your seams and stitches should be on the inside now.

6   Finally, tie both ends of the string together into a knot.

7   Fill with loose tea, grab a biscuit and your favourite mug and enjoy your cuppa with an eco-conscious conscience. If you use milk in your tea, handwash the teabag straight after use. If not, it'll need a wash every two to three uses.

SUSTAINABLE SWAPS:
The kitchen edition

When you're keen to keep the kitchen clean, hygienic and organized, it can be tempting to keep consuming single-use plastic. However, there are so many alternatives, and it's great to reduce, reuse and recycle with these little swaps.

- Instead of purchasing brand new plastic food storage containers, reuse what you've got. Plastic boxes from takeaways are great for storing food and empty (clean) jars hold more than you think, and most are freezable!

- Is your kitchen swimming in silicone? There's no need to throw out perfectly good utensils. Instead of purchasing more silicone spatulas and serving spoons, try switching to bamboo.

- If your local supermarket is a bit further afield, instead of driving there, opt in for home delivery. It's sort of like the grocery shopping version of public transport, and it means you get to spend more time at home. Sounds like a win-win.

- Try making swaps in your diet. Studies have shown that going plant-based is the "single biggest way" to stay on Mother Nature's good side. Cutting our meat and dairy consumption can totally slash our environmental impact, so even if it's only one night a week, why not give veganism a go?

LOW-WASTE FOOD SHOPPING

These days, it seems like purchasing food and plastic go hand in hand. In 2018, supermarkets sold UK shoppers approximately 58 billion plastic packets containing food. It's really difficult to completely cut plastic from your food shopping given how much of it is around, but, as with any eco-friendly lifestyle change, every little helps.

Try taking your own carrier bag, grab loose vegetables instead of pre-packaged (it'll save you having leftover food, too!), and swap food in plastic bags for food in cardboard, tins or jars.

Re-usable bag to the rescue!

TOP TIPS:
Eco-friendly food shops

Did you know that there are hundreds of bulk-buying food shops selling unpackaged pasta, rice, flour and other dried goods? Not only could you save a lot of money on your food shop, it'll also save you and the planet fuel, packaging and time.

Even better than shopping locally, why not try actually growing your own food? You'll know that absolutely no carbon has been emitted in food transportation, and it'll be so satisfying to think that all of your veg came from your fingertips.

Shop locally. You'll completely slash your carbon footprint if you choose to shop from local farms instead of major supermarkets.

Top Tips:
In the kitchen

Think baking paper is compostable? Think again. It's usually coated in a waxy texture, rendering it non-recyclable. Why not switch to a reusable, washable, freezer- and ovenproof silicone baking sheet? It's cleaner, cost-effective and kind of cute!

Instead of throwing your veggies straight in the compost bin, chop them up into smaller pieces first and they'll decompose much faster. If you'd like to compost but are scared of the smell, keep them in a bag or jar and pop them in the freezer, then, when it's compost bin day, throw them away.

Use microwaves. They cook food much faster than ovens do and therefore use much less energy. Miele, AEG and Beko all rank pretty highly on the eco-friendly front, so you'll be the *crème-de-la-eco-crème*. Read on for a delicious microwave meal.

VEGAN MICROWAVE LASAGNE IN A MUG

There's nothing like a delicious Italian-inspired dish to warm the heart and soul, and this microwave-friendly lasagne recipe is absolutely no exception.

YOU WILL NEED:

- 2 dried lasagne sheets
- 175 ml (6 fl oz) water
- 1 tsp olive oil
- 5 tbsp pizza sauce or vegan bolognaise-style sauce
- 4 tbsp vegan ricotta cheese
- 3 tbsp fresh spinach
- 1 tbsp vegan grated cheese
- Fresh basil
- A 1200W microwave (if your microwave is a lower wattage, you might need to increase the cooking time)
- A mug
- A plate

METHOD:

1   Break up your lasagne sheets into little pieces and place them in a large, microwave-safe mug, then cover with your water and olive oil.

2   Microwave on full heat for 90 seconds, give it a stir, then microwave for another 90 seconds or until your pasta sheets are soft. Drain the water away after use and move the pasta from the mug to a plate.

3   Put 1 tbsp bolognaise-style sauce in the bottom of your mug, then add a layer of pasta pieces, a layer of spinach and a layer of vegan ricotta. Repeat until you've reached the top of the mug, then top with vegan cheese.

4   Return to the microwave and cook it for 2½–3 minutes or until piping hot.

5   Let it stand for a minute or two, then tuck in! Much tastier than noodles from a plastic cup.

PREVENTING FOOD WASTE

While we might think that food wastage begins and ends with what's on our plates, it's easy to forget that plenty of food goes off before we've even touched it, simply because we're incorrectly storing things!

Onions and tomatoes

A guaranteed conversation starter

- A lot of people have become accustomed to putting vegetables straight into the fridge, but it makes far more sense to keep certain veggies, such as tomatoes and onions, in the fruit bowl. You might find they taste sweeter, too.

- Instead of keeping bread in its plastic packaging, put it in a cloth bag before placing it in the bread bin. This will help absorb any moisture which might cause mould. If it starts getting a bit stale, place it in the freezer to keep it fresh – it's best to slice before freezing so you don't have to rely on your superstrength to cut through frozen bread!

- Although it's easier to store your crackers and biscuits in the packs they come in, store them in tins and they'll last much longer – wait until Christmas time and you're bound to get a few pretty tins for free!

SPICY FRENCH TOAST

Use up stale bread for this tasty breakfast treat. Add some honey and berries for extra sweetness.

INGREDIENTS

- 2 eggs, beaten

- 150 ml (5 fl oz) milk, warmed

- A pinch of ground cinnamon

- A pinch of ground nutmeg

- 2 slices of stale bread, cut into fingers

- 25 g (1 oz) unsalted butter

- Honey to serve (optional)

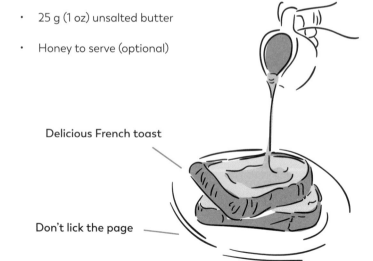

Delicious French toast

Don't lick the page

METHOD:

1   Mix the warm milk, eggs and spices together in a small saucepan.

2   Place the bread slices into a large, shallow dish and cover with the mixture. Leave to soak for 5 minutes.

3   Heat a frying pan and add the butter. When the butter is melted and beginning to froth, add the bread slices and fry until golden, turning frequently.

4   Drizzle with honey and serve immediately.

DONATING FOOD

It's not just clothes and furniture that charities accept; food banks are always looking for donations. If you've ever bought something in a hurry, realized it was the wrong item and chucked it out, remember you can always donate it. While it's always better to give non-perishable goods that you've bought new, some food banks accept food that's past its best-before-end date (BBE) as this isn't necessarily food that's "gone off".

If you do have food that's past its BBE, apps such as OLIO are designed for swapping and donating out-of-date food with others in your community. And don't forget, BBEs are guidelines. One UK supermarket is scrapping BBE dates on milk and asking for customers to apply the sniff test instead to stop food wastage. Just remember, if it's got green spots or is coated in white fur, best steer clear.

There's hope for these tins yet!

SUSTAINABLE FOOD STORAGE

Cut down on kitchenware. Instead of relying on giant kitchenware shops to provide you with storage containers, why not just reuse an old jar? There's nothing more homely looking than a pantry of jars filled with food, and you could even doodle your own labels on the outside – apply some blackboard paint and write what's inside, then you can wipe off if you need to. Most glass is also freezer-safe, so if you want to keep a second helping of last night's dinner in the freezer for next week, there's nothing to stop you!

Porridge oats

Pasta

Lentils

FANCY A FORAGE?

It's great having your own fruit at your fingertips by growing it in the garden, and shopping locally can bring you closer to your community, but there's nothing quite like getting back into nature by finding your own food. Picking blackberries and apples for a homemade crumble is ever so wholesome, and trying to make nettle soup from scratch is an adventure in itself, so why not give foraging a go? Before you touch anything unfamiliar, make sure you know *exactly* what it is by using plant identification books or apps, as not all plants are safe for human consumption!

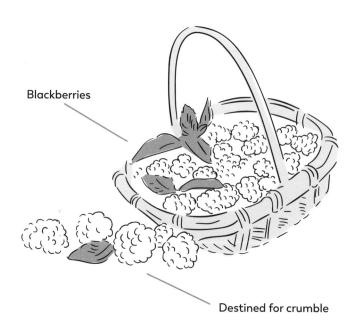

Blackberries

Destined for crumble

MIX UP YOUR FLOUR

It's easy to forget how many varieties of flour there are, given how standard using wheat has become. To help balance the soil and be fair to farmers, we can mix up the flour we use. Farmers tend to grow wheat, spelt, clover and rye in rotation, so try baking rye bread instead of your usual white loaf, or use coconut flour in your cookies. If farmers were to grow wheat exclusively, the soil would be totally devoid of nutrients and they'd have a tough time growing any crops at all.

Make it into bread, crackers, pasta or scones...

BATHROOM AND BEAUTY HACKS

Keeping clean and pristine is a sure-fire way to feel fabulous. The problem is that the planet disagrees with our demand for all those disposable products. Although we've all got our favourite plastic bottles full of potions, there are some amazing alternatives and you can make them yourself, too. From shampoo bars to toothpaste tablets, this chapter will show you how to maintain your health- and skin-care routine without harming the environment.

SUSTAINABLE SWAPS:
The bamboo edition

Bamboo is making a real splash in the beauty world. Give these easy swaps a try to slash your plastic usage.

🌿 Swap your plastic or electric toothbrush for a bamboo one with natural fibres. It'll take six months to decompose instead of a millennium, helping to really reduce your carbon footprint.

🌿 Swap plastic cotton buds for cardboard or bamboo ones, or, even better, why not try reusable swabs instead?

🌿 Once your hairbrush or comb has come to the end of its life, switch to bamboo alternatives that reduce hair breakage and won't end up in landfill.

SHAMPOO BAR FOR SENSITIVE SCALPS

Sensitive scalp? Give this DIY shampoo bar a go! The best part about this recipe is that you can use pretty much any essential oil you fancy – check the list below to see which is best for your hair type:

- **Normal:** cedarwood, eucalyptus, lavender, orange, rosemary

- **Oily:** basil, bergamot, cedarwood, grapefruit, lavender, lemon

- **Dry:** lavender, rosemary, sandalwood

- **Damaged:** lavender

- **Thinning:** basil, clary cage, rosemary, thyme, cedarwood

- **Flaky:** cedarwood, rosemary, sage, tea tree, thyme, patchouli

YOU WILL NEED:

- 30 g (1 oz) soap-free cleansing bar

- ½ tsp coconut oil

- 15 drops argan oil

- 10 drops essential oil (feel free to use a complementary combination)

METHOD:

1   Finely grate your "soap" bar.

2   Mix the grated soap and chopped herbs in a bowl and then add your coconut and essential oils.

3   Massage the mixture in your hands (you might want to pop on a pair of protective gloves for this bit) and knead it into a crumbly dough.

4   Press it firmly into the base of a muffin tray (silicone is great, but a metal tray greased with argan oil will work too!) and let it sit for a few hours.

5   Just like that, it's done! Your shampoo bar will keep for about a year.

Beautiful homemade shampoo

DIY DEODORANT

Wave goodbye to aerosol and roll-on deodorants with this simple recipe. This homemade deodorant will last you up to six months and will leave you smelling truly delicious.

YOU WILL NEED:

- 2.5 tbsp coconut oil
- 2.5 tbsp shea butter
- 30 g (1 oz) cornflour
- 1.5 tbsp baking soda
- 6 drops of lavender oil
- 6 drops of grapefruit oil
- 1 drop of tea tree oil

HOW TO USE:

- Splash or spritz your underarms with a bit of water.

- Scoop out a pea-sized amount of your deodorant and rub it between your fingers before applying to your underarms.

TIP: Your armpits might take a few weeks to adjust to the new product, so don't worry if it doesn't work straight away!

METHOD:

1   Put the coconut oil and shea butter in a glass bowl placed in a saucepan half filled with boiling water and put on the hob at a low–medium temperature, making sure the water doesn't spill into the bowl.

2   Keep stirring the coconut oil and shea butter until it's completely melted.

3   Add the remaining ingredients and mix it all together.

4   Pour into a smaller jar and let it cool down, then pop it in the fridge and let it solidify.

5   Either screw a lid back on, or, if you don't have a lid, cover with fabric tied with string.

MAKE YOUR OWN COTTON PADS

Cotton wool is like glitter, but fluffier. It gets stuck all over the place, even in our waterways! It's great at removing make-up, but the environmental impact simply isn't worth it. Why not try making these simple reusable cotton rounds instead? This method will allow you to make four pads, but it's super easy to scale up.

YOU WILL NEED:

- A small tumbler

- An old (clean) flannel, microfibre cloth or bath towel

- Thick embroidery thread and a needle

- Scissors and some sewing pins

- Two jars

Blanket stitch: easy when you know how

METHOD:

1   Draw eight circles (using the base of your glass as a template) onto your fabric then cut each circle out.

2   Lay two of your fabric circles on top of each other and pin together.

3   Blanket stitch (following the diagram if you're unfamiliar) around the edge to join the two pieces together.

4   Boom, you're done! Make as many as required, store your clean pads in one jar, and the used ones in another jar to keep them together. Before washing in the machine, put them in a mesh bag to protect them.

SUSTAINABLE SHEET MASK

Sheet masks are terrible for the planet *and* the bank account. The good thing is, they're really pretty simple to DIY...

Make a cup of green tea, add in a few drops of your favourite serums and essential oils then give it a stir.

While the tea brews, cut a face-shaped mask out of an old (but clean!) T-shirt or flannel. Soak it in the tea, leave it for about 10 minutes and then place on your face.

After use, rinse it in the sink and hang to dry. Zero waste, glowing skin!

Sustainable
sheet mask

Good for your skin and the planet!

HOMEMADE MAKE-UP REMOVER

Make-up removal wipes are *très* eco-unfriendly, and biodegradable alternatives are *très* pricey. What's the alternative? Bottles upon bottles of micellar cleansing water? No thanks, this homemade remover sounds *much* better.

In a small jar with a screw cap lid, add ½ tsp baby shampoo, 1 tsp melted coconut oil and fill to the top with water. Pop your lid on, give it a shake and your make-up remover is complete! These work brilliantly alongside your homemade cotton pads, and it'll keep things super planet-friendly.

You'll never guess what's in here

Make-up Remover

DIY SHOWER PUFF

Shower puffs, scrubs, scrunchies, whatever you want to call them, are brilliant companions when it comes to exfoliation. The problem is, unless you're willing to fork out for a biodegradable version – or even an organic loofah – there aren't many sustainable alternatives. By making this super-simple shower scrunchie, you'll be keeping the planet (and your skin) perfectly clean.

YOU WILL NEED:

- Hessian fabric (an old sack will do), cut into a rectangle measuring 12×75 cm (5×29½ in.)

- A heavy-duty needle and thick thread (a darning needle and embroidery thread will work)

- Approximately 40 cm (16 in.) ribbon

- Sewing pins

- Safety pin

This will keep you squeaky clean

METHOD:

1 Turn the short edges of the fabric in by 1 cm (⅜ in.) and secure with stitches to create a hem.

2 Stitch the long sides together and turn your hessian tube inside out, so the seams are on the inside.

3 Attach a closed safety pin to the end of your ribbon then pull it through your hessian tube while keeping hold of the pinless end to ensure you don't lose it.

4 You should notice that there's a lot more fabric than ribbon, so, as you pull the ribbon through, the hessian should start to bunch up, forming a scrunchie.

5 Tie the ends of your ribbon together as close to the scrunchie as possible, then tie another knot, securing the ends of the ribbon to each other, making a loop.

6 And it's done! Wash in the machine with your clothes whenever you need to and be amazed at how long it'll last you.

SUSTAINABLE SWAPS:
The bathroom edition

Bits and bobs from the bathroom are always ending up in the bin. Minimize your eco-impact with these simple swaps that mean you can keep your creature comforts while keeping the planet happy.

- Swap disposable razors for either a metal or bamboo razor with a replaceable head. You'll minimize your waste and they're usually much better quality, too!

- If you're someone who has a menstrual cycle, it might be a good idea to try swapping from regular sanitary towels or tampons to washable period pants or pads or a menstrual cup. Say goodbye to overflowing bathroom bins!

- Instead of buying brand new fiddly bottles of hand wash every time you run out, try using refill packs instead – they use around 75 per cent less plastic, are fully recyclable and usually work out cheaper, too. Alternatively, go old school with a standard bar of soap; read on for a fab soap-dish craft involving repurposed chopsticks.

HOMEMADE WHITENING TOOTHPASTE

It's so important we care for our pearly whites, and there's no reason we can't do that while caring for the planet, too.

Thoroughly mix 4 tbsp melted coconut oil, 10 drops of peppermint oil, 2 tbsp baking soda and 1 tsp activated charcoal powder in a little airtight jar. Scoop out a regular toothpaste-sized amount and apply to your toothbrush to use. Brush as usual and you'll have clean white teeth and a conscience to match!

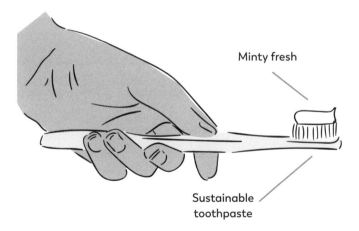

Minty fresh

Sustainable
toothpaste

Note: Make sure not to ingest this toothpaste, and consider speaking to your dentist before making any significant changes to your routine.

CHOPSTICK SOAP DISH

Whether you opt for pho, noodles or ramen, there's no doubt that Asian cuisine is divine, but it tends to leave the cutlery drawer overflowing with chopsticks. This simple hack will help you transform your chopsticks into a cute soap dish!

YOU WILL NEED:

· 12 chopsticks

· Thick thread

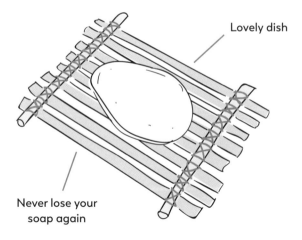

Lovely dish

Never lose your
soap again

METHOD

1   Lay ten chopsticks down horizontally in front of you leaving a 0.5-cm (⅛-in.) gap in between each one.

2   Place two chopsticks on top of them, vertically and 1 cm (⅜ in.) from the edge.

3   Wrap some thick thread around the right-hand vertical chopstick and the top of the horizontal chopsticks, then keep wrapping around in a criss-cross motion until it's fixed securely in place. Repeat, moving down the chopsticks, one side at a time.

4   There you have it! Your very own zero-waste soap dish.

TOP TIPS:
For skincare

Adding used coffee grounds to a little melted coconut oil makes a perfectly natural exfoliant.

No need to waste money and plastic on hand cream with this handy hack. Heat 600 ml (20 fl oz) whole milk and pour into a bowl. Once the milk is lukewarm, soak your hands in it for 10 minutes and they'll feel nourished and silky smooth!

Dark circles under your eyes? Instead of trying disposable, silicone eye patches, simply crush up a few mint leaves, lie down and place them under your eyes for 10 minutes. Wipe the leaves away then rinse your face with warm water.

Coconut oil makes an excellent cuticle moisturizer to help keep your digits hydrated.

Try switching to cruelty-free cosmetic brands, whether that's shampoo, make-up or even hand sanitizer – look out for the little bunny on the packaging which indicates that no new animal tests were carried out in the making of the product.

Save condiment jars and use them to store make-up brushes, bamboo "cotton" buds or your new homemade skincare products.

Avoid any skincare products containing palm oil, as obtaining palm oil destroys natural habitats and makes animals such as orang-utans, elephants and rhinos homeless due to its reliance on mass deforestation.

Swimming in the sea wearing sun cream can be really damaging to sea life, so check your sunscreen is "reef-safe" before purchasing.

SUSTAINABLE SKIN SCRUB

There's no scent quite as refreshing as cucumber and mint, so what better way to kickstart your day than with this homemade exfoliating scrub?

Mix 200 g (7 oz) sugar, 235 ml (8 fl oz) olive oil, 10 drops cucumber oil and 10 drops peppermint oil in a bowl, and that's it! Easy, right? Transfer it into an airtight jar and keep it in the bathroom. This scrub might be abrasive on the face, but it's perfect for exfoliating your body, although keep it away from sensitive areas as the mint can sting a little!

Refreshing skin scrub

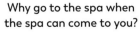

Why go to the spa when the spa can come to you?

DIY DRY SHAMPOO

Greasy hair, who cares? Nobody should, but if it bothers you and you're looking for a quick, eco-friendly fix, give this super-simple hack a go.

Mix 2 tbsp cornflour and 2 tbsp of one of the below ingredients, then add 6 drops of essential oil and mix – you can use whichever scent you prefer. Transfer to an airtight jar and apply to greasy roots using a make-up brush then comb through.

- **Blonde:** More cornflour

- **Strawberry blonde/red:** Cinnamon

- **Medium brown:** Cocoa powder

- **Grey:** Arrowroot powder or cornflour (if you have grey/blue tones, add a little activated charcoal powder)

- **Dark brown:** Cocoa powder and activated charcoal powder (1 tbsp each)

- **Black:** Activated charcoal powder

MAKE YOUR OWN SHAVING GEL

If you shave, the chances are that your shaving cream comes in an aerosol can. These can be super harmful to the planet, from the toxic chemicals to the non-recyclable cans. For an eco-friendly alternative, why not make it yourself?

Combine 4 tbsp aloe vera gel, 1 tsp melted coconut oil, ½ tsp vegetable glycerine, 1 tsp jojoba oil, 3 drops cedarwood oil and 3 drops orange oil in a shallow jar. To use it, just scoop a little out and spread it on wet skin for a silky-smooth shave!

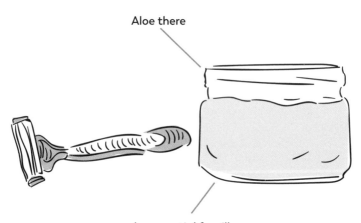

Aloe there

An essential for silky smooth skin

UPCYCLE THOSE SPONGES

It's great to switch old habits for new, planet-friendly alternatives, but doing that *and* limiting waste can be tricky. For example, now that you've made some homemade dish scrubbers (page 16), you're probably wondering what you should do with all of those disposable sponges you've got lying around. Well, if you cut them up, stuff them in the base of a shallow jar and then dowse them in nail polish remover, you can make your own little nail polish remover pot! Simple and effective, not to mention travel-friendly!

Add a few drops

Press nail into the sponge

WARDROBE HACKS

Whether you're a trendsetter or have had the same wardrobe of clothes for 20 years, there's bound to be something for you in this section. Here you'll find tips on creating a capsule wardrobe, upcycling the garments you don't wear anymore and transforming second-hand shopping from a total drag into your latest hobby.

DITCH FAST FASHION

Let's start with some cold facts. Did you know that 93 per cent of fast fashion brands don't pay their workers a living wage? What about the fact that the production of textiles contributes more to climate change than international flights and shipping combined? And it might also shock you (or it might not) to find out that three in five garments from fast fashion shops end up in landfill. It's pretty scary stuff, so the first major hack for living a more planet-friendly lifestyle is simple: ditch fast fashion. Now, let's find out how to build a wonderful wardrobe without it.

BUILD A
CAPSULE WARDROBE

Capsule wardrobes are all about scrapping fads and microtrends and opting for a selection of sustainable garments that can be worn in loads of different ways. This is just a whistle-stop tour, but building a capsule wardrobe is effectively about making mindful choices instead of impulse buying. But how do you actually create one?

1   Firstly, consider what clothes you *need*. Do you work out a lot? Does your job require some sort of uniform? If you have garments that are necessities, they're exempt from the capsule wardrobe.

2   Next step: plan. What colour scheme are you going for? It's best to go for neutral colours (think whites, blacks, greys, beiges and pastels), then you can pick a few bolder colours for expressing yourself. Then think of shapes: what style of jeans do you prefer, and do you prefer round- or V-neck tops?

3   Now that you have a plan, sustainably remove everything else from your wardrobe, i.e. sell or donate, upcycle or repurpose just don't throw away!

A GENDER-NEUTRAL STARTING POINT:

- Five T-shirts (basic colours)
- Two formal shirts or blouses
- A well-made jacket (if you're after denim or leather, make sure it's thrifted!)
- A blazer
- Two pairs of smart trousers
- Two pairs of jeans
- Three jumpers or cardigans
- Two "trendy" pieces per season
- Two hoodies
- Two pairs of lounge trousers
- A pair of black or brown boots
- A pair of sandals
- A pair of white trainers
- A pair of smart shoes

THE DOs AND DON'Ts OF DONATION

You've cleared out your wardrobe and sold some things on social media, now the rest is going to charity. There's just one problem... if you can't sell your own clothes, what makes you think that a charity shop can? Oxfam announced that over 70 per cent of donated clothes end up in landfill in Africa, totalling at least 450,000 kg of garments *a week*!

REMEMBER

Instead of just assuming that charity shops will take what you don't want, read on to ensure that what you donate won't be binned.

- **DO:** Wash before you donate! It seems obvious but it's a step that many skip.

- **DON'T:** Donate something damaged or stained. Try to mend it first, but if you can't, use the fabric for a DIY project.

- **DO:** Go to a physical charity shop instead of a clothing bank. They're more likely to need all the clothes they can get.

- **DON'T:** Assume they'll take the garments. Some charities only accept certain things, so don't go breaking their rules or they'll be left with the burden of your old undies.

- **DO:** Try downloading reGAIN, the app that works with British Red Cross to give even damaged clothes a second life. You simply download a free label, take your garments to a drop-off point and they're donated to a charity of your choice or repaired and resold! Nike recycle old trainers (and turn them into playgrounds for kids!), and Schuh recycle any old shoes. And for a real win-win, you get a discount on your next purchase with most of these schemes, too.

HOW TO FALL IN LOVE WITH THRIFTING

Thrifting sounds cool. Some people create the impression it's a haven where you get designer pieces for pennies and fur coats practically free. However, the reality is that it can often be pretty overwhelming, especially if it's new to you. Try these steps to help you adjust to the wonderful world of thrifting.

Vintage jacket waiting to be found

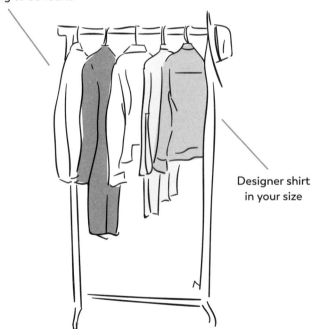

Designer shirt in your size

- Firstly, instead of rifling through every single rail at a charity shop, skim-read the room. Are there any patterns you're instantly drawn to? Any particular colours? Do you need jeans or a coat? Pick something to look for, and you'll be less likely to get overwhelmed or impulse buy.

- Next, see the potential. These garments are at least second-hand, so the quality will rarely be as it was new. However, if you imagine how it would look after a wash, an extra button or some new embroidery on the cuff, then you might just get somewhere.

- Finally, be patient and have fun! Rummaging through charity-shop rails is the direct opposite of fast fashion. It takes time, but it can be really rewarding when you find the perfect piece or grab a beautiful bargain.

FINDING VINTAGE GEMS

Vintage and retro shops are often home to some high quality, one-of-a-kind pieces, created long before the days of fast fashion. While some "vintage kilo sales" might just sell old pieces for a great price, there are some vintage shops which specialize in reworking old pieces. These shops, like WeAreCow, turn vintage designer men's shirts into stunning ladies' dresses, and old unwanted jeans into beautiful dungarees. If you're not crafty (and don't fancy learning how to sew) then these might be the shops for you. If, however, you love getting your sewing machine out, read on for some handy upcycles!

MAKE YOUR OWN 50:50 CLOTHES

One way of ensuring your garments are totally unique is by mashing them together, yep, literally!

Take two of the same garments that you're bored of wearing and cut them both in half. You can cut them horizontally, vertically or diagonally, just make sure you cut both pieces in the exact same place and way. Now it's time to swap each half over. Pin the new garment together (keeping the top and back layer separate), then turn it inside out and stitch the halves together. Flip it the right way round and your quirky new piece is ready to wear.

Same-but-different

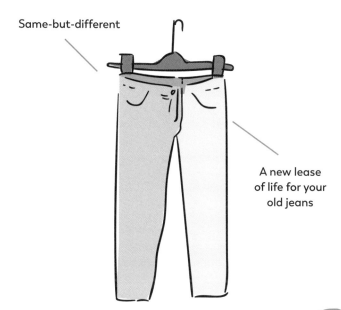

A new lease of life for your old jeans

TOP TIPS:
For your wardrobe

Every time we wash acrylic and polyester garments, microplastics are released into our waterways and eventually end up in the ocean. Try to purchase 100 per cent cotton and linen fabrics, and if you do find yourself with any acrylic or polyester garments, limit the amount you wash them as much as possible.

Skip fur, unless it's second-hand. Faux fur is a huge emitter of microplastics and a burden on the planet, but it's considerably better than fur-farming. So, if you can get your hands on second-hand fur then it's probably more eco-friendly than its faux counterpart.

Instead of being thrown out, old bed covers can be repurposed in many ways, from dust sheets to a new set of pyjamas; so, if you or a friend is creative, it might be worth keeping them by.

If you've got lots of used scented candles around, place them (unlit!) in the back of your drawers and wardrobes to keep your clothes smelling superb.

Try alternative fabrics – advances have been made in the use of natural fibre types, such as bamboo, hemp and nettle, which perform well compared to the more widely used textiles. Some brands are also recycling water bottles into polyester for clothing – just look on the labels for "100-per-cent recycled polyester" or "made with partially recycled materials".

Buy brands that accept their products back for repair, if damaged, and that are willing to recycle if garments are returned to them after years of use.

Take care of your clothes so that they last. Be extra careful when washing delicate items by putting them in separate fabric bags or by placing your items in pillowcases and knotting them closed. Store items properly too – clothes that are scrunched up and wedged into drawers and cupboards are unlikely to be worn or last well. Fold or roll smaller items and store them upright in drawers so you can see them all at once.

If you do buy clothes online, make the most sustainable choices you can. For instance, standard delivery will have a smaller carbon footprint than speedy delivery – and click and collect will be even lower (zero if you are able to walk or cycle!).

NATURAL TIE-DYE

Wild dyeing is a cheap and fun way to breathe new life into your clothes. Anything can be used to create a natural dye, from onion skins and cabbage leaves to berries, bark and other foraged finds. Play safe with your choice of plant, though – don't use anything that is known to be poisonous or an irritant. Do your research first.

YOU WILL NEED:

- Bucket
- Clothing made of natural fibres
- Large old saucepan or cooking pot with a lid (you won't want to use it for cooking after this!)
- Mordant (this is fixative, necessary to hold the colours. Alum is best and can be found in supermarkets as it's often used as a preservative, but if you want to go au naturel, lemon juice or white wine vinegar will do the job)
- Rubber gloves
- Elastic bands or twine
- Apron
- Your choice of non-poisonous plant for dyeing
- Wooden spoon

Cute onion-skin tie-dye

Is there nothing an onion can't do?

METHOD:

1   Soak the item to be dyed in a bucket of cold water for an hour.

2   Once the hour is up, fill an old saucepan with water and heat until it's on a rolling boil. Add your mordant of choice. Ratios will vary but use 1 tsp of mordant per litre (1.75 pt) of water as a general guide. Stir until it dissolves.

3   Add the fabric and turn down the heat, place the lid on the pot and leave to simmer for two hours. Then remove from the heat and allow to cool.

4   Take out the fabric while wearing rubber gloves. Rinse it in cold running water and allow to dry on a washing line. When dry, use elastic bands or twine to tie knots in your garment. Experiment with your own knots or find inspiration for particular patterns online.

5   Next, create the dye by adding your plant material to the cleaned pot and enough water to cover the plants. Add your prepared fabric and slowly bring the water to the boil. Then turn down the heat, cover and simmer for an hour, stirring occasionally with a wooden spoon. Check the colour every so often by lifting the fabric. Remember the shade will be significantly paler once the fabric has dried.

6   When you are happy with the colour, turn off the heat and allow the fabric to soak in the dye until cool. Take out your fabric and rinse in cold running water. Allow to dry.

7   Wash your hand-dyed items separately when washing for the first time, just in case the dye hasn't set sufficiently.

UPCYCLE A BASIC TEE INTO A CUTE CROP TOP

This fun hack will breathe new life into an old T-shirt.

YOU WILL NEED:

- An old T-shirt
- Chalk (a different colour to the fabric)
- Scissors (or a rotary cutter and mat)
- Ruler
- Sewing machine
- Seam ripper
- Needle and thread

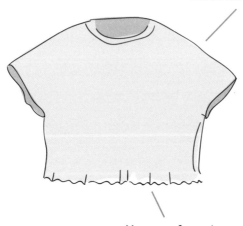

Saved from landfill

Your new favourite top

METHOD:

1   While wearing the t-shirt, make a small mark where you'd like it cropped to.

2   Take off the T-shirt, turn it inside out and lay it down flat, front facing you.

3   Around 1.5 cm below your mark, draw a straight horizontal line with your chalk across the whole width of the top, then cut along the line. Cut the hem off both sleeves.

4   Roll the raw edges (the sleeves and bottom of the top) in by a few millimetres twice and pull them taught to stretch the edges slightly. Then use your machine to zig-zag stitch, to create a frilly "lettuce" hem.

5   Turn the right way round, snip any excess threads and you're done!

PRETTY IN PINK

Ever accidentally turned an entire white wash a horrifying marshmallow pink? You're not the only one! However, with this avocado hack the goal is actually to turn your white garments a stunning shade of shell pink.

YOU WILL NEED:

- A large kitchen pot

- Laundry detergent

- Four (clean) avocado skins and stones (the more you use the darker the colour)

- Plain white linen or cotton fabric

- A wooden spoon

METHOD:

1   Gently wash the garments you wish to dye in a pot of hot water and laundry detergent, then leave to soak overnight. TIP: Dye as many as you can in one go to minimize the amount of energy you're using.

2   The next day, rinse out the pot and refill with hot water – you need enough for the fabric to be able to move when submerged.

3   Add all of your avocado stones, bring the pot to the boil, then reduce to a simmer. The avocado stones should first go pink, then maroon over the course of around 40 minutes.

4   Now, add your fabric to the pot and give it a good stir. Leave it on the heat for a further hour or two then remove and let it sit in the pot overnight. The longer it soaks, the brighter the pink will be.

5   When you're happy with the shade, remove it from the pot and rinse it in cool water and fabric soap and hang to dry.

6   That's it! You're now able to transform anything boring and blank into a pretty salmon pink.

MINDFUL SHOPPING

If you thought you'd left algebra back in middle school then think again, it's formula time.

Working out how much a garment costs per wear will lead to a much more cost- and planet-friendly way of shopping.

COST OF PIECE
÷
NUMBER OF WEARS
=
COST PER WEAR

Working out how many times you'll wear a piece might take a bit of guesswork but try to be as realistic as possible! Consider which of your coveted garments have the best cost-per-wear ratio, then ask yourself a few questions:

- Does this fill me with joy?

- Is it practical?

- Is it made from natural fabric?

- Is it timeless or just trendy?

- Can I dress it up/down?

- How can I style this without purchasing something else to match?

- Will I wear this ten times in the next three months?

By taking an extra few seconds to think before making each purchase, you'll help to reduce the amount of unworn clothing in your wardrobe and therefore limit how much you're getting rid of!

MINIMIZING
TEXTILE WASTE

If you've taken on the challenge of creating a capsule wardrobe (page 74), you're probably wondering how to sustainably sell your old clothes. There are so many online marketplaces, from the beautifully basic bidding site eBay, to the ever so edgy Depop that's great for selling upcycles. Sites like Vestiaire are full of high-end pieces that get verified before you sell, so it's a great platform for any rare or designer pieces you are ready to part with. Try to sell locally to minimize how far your parcels travel, and recycle plastic bags for packaging. Alternatively, there's nothing quite like a car boot sale.

DIY HACKS

Doing it yourself is in. These clever DIY hacks and crafts will have you transforming your house in no time, whether it's making old plastic bottles into chic plant pots or turning rags into rugs, you can guarantee your home is one-of-a-kind.

DISPLAY-WORTHY STORAGE BOXES

Is your home overflowing with cardboard boxes? While cardboard is probably the easiest material to recycle, not all of it actually gets recycled. Instead of chucking it, why not upcycle it to make handy storage boxes for blankets and bedding?

YOU WILL NEED:

- Cardboard box

- Contact adhesive or hot glue gun

- Sisal rope

- An old cushion cover

Miscellaneous stuff never looked so good

Rope-covered box

METHOD:

1. Remove the top flaps from your box, then cover the lower eighth of your box's four external sides in contact adhesive (or use a hot glue gun) but leave the base of the box untouched. Wrap a long length of sisal rope around the box, holding it firmly in place to help it stick, and adding more glue as you go further up the box.

2. Keep wrapping the rope around until you reach the top of the box. Then, turn an old cushion cover inside out, and, pinching the corners on the inside, place it into the box and fold the opening over the edges. It should be quite tight and stay in place, but if it's loose, use a dab of fabric glue to keep it stuck.

3. You're all done! This is a super-easy make to scale up or down and can be used for storing just about anything.

FROM BOOK TO PICTURE FRAME

Now, don't go chopping up this book before you've finished reading the rest of these nifty hacks, but making your own picture frame using this book – or any other book for that matter – is a great way to add character to your living space. This easy idea will get you moving your photos from your phone to your mantelpiece in no time.

YOU WILL NEED:

- A photo

- This book (or another book!)

- A pencil

- A metal ruler

- A craft knife

- A cutting mat

- Scissors

- Acid-free masking tape

METHOD:

1   Lay your photo over your book, and very lightly draw around the edge. Remove the picture then draw another rectangle about 0.5 cm (⅛ in.) inside the other.

2   Place the book on a cutting mat, open out the cover, then cut the inside rectangle out of the cover using your metal ruler and craft knife.

3   Put your photo inside with the picture facing outward, and if it's landscape ensure that it's the right way round when the spine faces up.

4   Secure on the inside using masking tape, and it should look so quaint that you can't wait to make more! Charity shops are full of hundreds of old hardback books, so start collecting.

MAKE YOUR OWN RAG RUG

Rugs are a lovely way to keep your toes snuggly and to warm up a space, but they're really rather expensive. However, it's super cheap (or even free!), easy and eco-friendly to make your own from some of your unwanted clothes; so have a clear-out then get crafty for this rag rug. If you use old towels instead of clothes, you can make a cute bathmat instead!

YOU WILL NEED:

- Loads of old clothes you don't mind chopping up (T-shirts, jeans and jumpers are great for this, but avoid shiny or scratchy fabric, as uncomfortable toes are no joke)

- Large bulldog clips

- Scissors

- Needle and thread

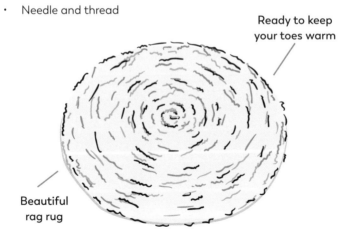

Ready to keep
your toes warm

Beautiful
rag rug

METHOD:

1   Cut your garments into as many 3-cm-wide (1⅛-in.) strips as you can.

2   With your bulldog clips, attach the ends of three strands to a flat surface (a desk or even a cutting mat would work), then create a standard braid. Once you've reached the end of one piece of fabric, add another piece in its place so you can create one continuous braid.

3   Now, coil the braid in on itself to make a tight, snail-shell spiral. Stitch it a few times to ensure it doesn't unravel.

4   Repeat until you're happy with the size of your round rug and, yippee, you're done!

THE POWER OF PAINT: CHAIRS

Have you ended up with furniture that just doesn't fit your aesthetic, but don't want to waste a perfectly good item? Here's how to upgrade an old fabric chair or sofa without the need for expensive upholstery. NOTE: The finer and smoother the fabric of your furniture, the more like leather it will look.

Simply grab a medium-sized decorating brush, dip it in water, get the surface of the chair slightly wet then paint the cover using a water-based chalk paint. Make sure you're starting with a really thin wash and be patient – this will take a good few coats which each require drying time in between, and for a really smooth result it's good to sand with a medium sanding block after each layer has dried. Brush in different directions to really get into the texture.

Last season's chair, this season's colour

THE POWER OF PAINT: DRESSERS

Purchasing second-hand furniture is cheaper and more sustainable, but it's also a bit daunting. Most of what's in charity shops can seem outdated or simply boring, but with a lick of paint and some new handles you can make *anything* fit your aesthetic! Here are a few pointers to get you started on upcycling a dresser.

Firstly, sand it down, then give it a good clean to remove any dust. Next, decide whether you want to keep the grain of the wood visible; will you use stain or paint? Stain will allow the natural wood to shine through, whereas paint will allow for colour-popping creativity. A good mix and match of the two can work really well. If you're using paint, make sure you're going in with thin layers, and sanding down after each layer has dried to get a smooth, sleek finish. Finally, replace the handles if desired. Some dressers come with stunning brass handles, but some look dated and dull! Replacing handles and knobs with modern alternatives from the local DIY shop will truly transform your furniture. Congrats, you've taken an old dresser from drab to fab!

UPCYCLING LAMP BASES

Do you have childhood figurines that you can't bear to part with? With this easy hack, you can transform cherished toys into a fun lamp before they end up in landfill.

YOU WILL NEED:

- Your beloved childhood figurines (plastic toys work best)

- Sticky tack

- Contact adhesive

- An old lamp with a relatively long stem

- Single colour spray paint (choose according to the room your lamp will be in; gold works a treat in most spaces)

Cherished childhood toys

Incredibly chic lamp

METHOD:

1   Unplug your lamp, remove the lampshade and bulb, and arrange your toys around the stem, temporarily sticking them on with sticky tack. Try to arrange the figures in varying heights and in different poses to create a scene.

2   Once you're satisfied with the arrangement, swap the sticky tack for contact adhesive on each figurine, one by one – remember, once this stuff is stuck, it's *stuck*, there's no going back!

3   Wait for the adhesive to finish drying, then spray the whole lamp stem, base and figurines the colour of your choosing and leave to dry – make sure you don't spray any of the electric parts of the lamp!

4   When dry, pop your bulb and lampshade on, plug in and switch on. Cool, right?

DIY DRAUGHT EXCLUDER

While new builds are good at retaining heat, older houses aren't as draughtproof. This simple DIY will help protect your doorways from draughts and keep your house warmer.

YOU WILL NEED:

- An old pair of jeans

- Old stray socks or laddered tights

- Scissors

- A needle and thread

- Adhesive Velcro patches (optional)

TIP: If you're unsure about the aesthetic of the spare-leg-on-the-floor draught excluder, cover it with the sleeve of an old jumper, or decorate however you fancy!

METHOD:

1   Cut one of the legs off an old pair of jeans, keeping the rest for stuffing, turn the leg inside out and then tightly stitch the ankle closed. Sew along the length of the leg to make a rectangle if one side is slanted, then trim any excess fabric – also keep this to use as stuffing!

2   Turn the jean leg the right way round and stuff it firmly with your leftover jeans (cut into strips), old socks, tights, scraps of fabric and anything else you've got that's soft, warm and out of use.

3   Once it's stuffed full, sew the other end of your jean leg together.

4   If you want the excluder protecting a particular cold spot, spread three pieces of Velcro evenly along the denim sausage, peel off the other side, then press it firmly against the very bottom of your door so it's touching the ground.

5   Enjoy the difference it makes and create one for every room in the house to reap all the benefits.

FROM PLASTIC BOTTLE TO PENCIL CASE

These easy no-sew pencil cases will keep your stationery organized and your recycling bin empty!

YOU WILL NEED:

- Plastic bottles (you'll need two per pencil case)

- Scissors and/or craft knife

- A zip the same length as the circumference of your bottle

- Hot glue gun

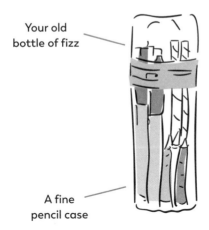

Your old bottle of fizz

A fine pencil case

METHOD:

1 Carefully cut the top few inches off one bottle where the neck begins to narrow, and cut the bottom few inches off your other bottle.

2 Wrap the zip around the lip of the inside of your longer bottle, making sure the correct side is facing outward. Ensure the zip is far enough away from the bottle lip that it can move freely, then glue in place. TIP: Hot glue guns can be a tad messy, so ensure you don't get glue in the zip's teeth!

3 Once one side of your zip is glued down, repeat on the other side with the shorter bottle end, making sure it's perfectly lined up.

4 Wait for the glue to dry, pop your pencils and pens in and you're all finished! Easy, right?

UPCYCLED CANDLE JARS

Candles make gorgeous gifts, but scented candles in particular are really damaging to the planet. They release greenhouse gases, and are made using petroleum, a non-renewable resource. Instead, try making your own candle jars like these – perfect decorations and presents that can be reused again and again.

Bringer of
Christmas cheer

Epsom salts

SNOW GLO(W)BE

Coat the outside of an old large jar in white glue, then roll the jar in Epsom salts. Wrap a festive ribbon around the neck and pop a pillar candle in. When lit up, it should look like a glowing snowball!

ALL THAT GLITTERS

Wrap masking tape around the jar about two thirds of the way down, then coat the bottom third in glue. Sprinkle biodegradable glitter all over the lower section and wait for it to dry. Then, peel off the masking tape and brush off any excess glitter. When lit, it should sparkle like a little disco ball! As you get more adventurous with this hack, try making different shapes with the masking tape to create glowing windows in the glass.

TOP TIPS:
In the home

Old masking tape is a nightmare to peel. Try putting your roll of tape in the microwave next to a glass of water, and zap it for 15 seconds. It should feel quite warm, and should now work as good as new!

If you have leftover paint from a DIY project, you risk it drying out by leaving it in the tin can with those pesky lids that never seem to close (or open!). Pour leftover paint into an airtight mason jar and store in a cool dry place to save for any future touch-ups.

Wondering what to do with those paintless cans? Cover an old, clean tin can in paint, and when it's dry you can use it as a little plant pot for herbs or succulents!

Minimize your waste the best you can by turning any scraps of wood into your own mini crafts, such as little Christmas tree ornaments or coasters.

Use wallpaper left over from redecorating for matching drawer liners or wrapping paper.

If you've got leftover fabric, use it as stuffing for another craft, or turn it into a patchwork quilt.

Instead of throwing out a pencil when it gets short, use a few stray pen lids to extend it. Simply stack a few old ballpoint pen caps on the end of your pencil to make it longer and lengthen its life, too.

SUSTAINABLE SWAPS:
The DIY edition

Give these simple swaps a go to make your DIY projects as planet-friendly as possible.

🍃 Avoid resin when you craft! Resin art is trendy, but if you get bored of it, sadly it'll just end up in landfill as most of it isn't eco-friendly. Instead, opt for glass or biodegradable alternatives.

🍃 Instead of purchasing eco-unfriendly wood varnish, try using natural furniture stain or shellac coatings. They're free of harsh chemicals, and they're still food-prep friendly! If applying to high-use areas, such as kitchen counters, add a water-based sealant over the varnish to make it more durable.

🍃 When upcycling, consider all the craft products and materials you use and try to switch to more eco-friendly versions.

🍃 Instead of chucking it, fix it! There are millions of videos on the internet, and if you're looking in the right place then you're bound to find one of someone repairing something you've broken. If not, sell it for parts – somebody will want it.

SUSTAINABLE FURNITURE

Here are a few tips to help you make the most planet-friendly choice when it comes to picking new furniture:

- A new piece of furniture for you doesn't necessarily mean that it has to be brand new. Look around second-hand furniture stores, online auction sites, flea markets and car boot fairs and see if there's something that fits the bill. You can often find high-value items with little wear for a fraction of the retail price if you're prepared to look for them.

- If it must be new, delve into the sustainability and environmental practices of the companies that you plan to purchase your items from. Look for a Forest Stewardship Council (FSC) label.

- Avoid furniture made from tropical hardwood or other non-sustainable sources, unless it's second-hand.

- Buy furniture that will last. It may cost more, but see it as an investment and a way to play your part in creating a sustainable future. Cheap, mass-produced furniture is designed to be thrown away after a few years, whereas a good-quality piece of furniture can last several lifetimes.

- Consider items made from reclaimed wood – wood that had a previous use, such as for floorboards or rafters.

REPURPOSING UNLOVED HOUSEHOLD OBJECTS

When we change up our décor, old furniture can be sold, donated or transformed – just like clothes. Here are a few ideas for how you can flip furniture on a budget.

FROM CURTAIN RAIL TO CLOTHES RACK

Try hanging two lengths of (strong) rope from your ceiling, create a loop at the end of each and slide in an old curtain rail. Hanging your clothes from the ceiling is a massive space saver, and will make for a quirky storage solution!

BOOK BOOKSHELVES

Secure two angle brackets to your wall, side by side, then top them with three hardback books (or however many it takes to cover the bracket). Voila! Your own little bookshelves that can be used for displaying more books, photos or flowers.

BEDSIDE TABLE

Repurpose an old wooden stool as a nightstand. Sand it down and give it a lick of paint to match your room. Tightly wrap twine between the two opposite footrests to create mini shelves, then you've got a lovely new bedside table!

BICYCLE PLANT STAND

Stand an old bike up using two bike stands, then spray the whole thing with a colour of your choice. If it has a basket, fill it with soil and your favourite flowers, and if not, attach a basket to the saddle or rear rack instead.

WINE BOTTLE CHIC

A used wine bottle is full of un-tapped potential. Once the bottle is clean and dry, you can turn it into a candle holder simply by pushing a long candle down into the top (you may want to bevel the edge so it fits more snugly). Once the candle is lit, allow the wax to run down the side for a characterful appearance. Alternatively, use the bottle as a vase for a few stems of leaves or flowers. You can choose whether to keep the label on or take it off, or why not try painting it with acrylic paint to create your very own piece of home decor?

FROM PAINTBRUSH TO DRAWER HANDLES

It's easy to wreck a perfectly good paintbrush by forgetting to clean it after a little DIY or upcycling. The best way to reduce waste is to soak your brushes in a jar of soapy water when you've finished painting, but if it's too late, an alternative is to upcycle!

If you want a crafty look, leave the bristles intact, but if you want something slightly sleeker, you can saw the bristles and metal casing off. Either way, this hack is simple.

YOU WILL NEED:

- An old paintbrush

- A drill

- Two long screws

- Two nuts that fit the screws

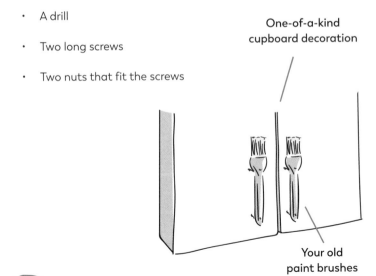

One-of-a-kind cupboard decoration

Your old paint brushes

METHOD:

1 Drill two holes at the top and bottom of the brush handle.

2 Measure the gap between the holes and drill two holes into the drawer, so that they're the same distance apart.

3 Insert two long screws through the paintbrush holes and drawer holes, and secure with two matching-sized nuts. Leave a gap of about 5 cm (2 in.) between the wood and the paintbrush for your hand, and that's it!

These work fabulously in an artsy space, but can blend seamlessly into a kitchen, too. Just remember that if the handle is likely to be getting wet, it's best to treat it with linseed oil or shellac.

GARDEN HACKS

Whether you're green-fingered or a total rookie, there's nothing that brings us closer to nature than gardening. In this section, you'll find ideas to help you bring nature indoors and to cultivate your own green area outside, no matter how big or small your garden is!

CLEAR THE AIR

We live in a world where it can be tricky to get access to clean air, given how just about everything seems to emit carbon dioxide. However, house plants are here to help! By keeping a few plants in your home, you can improve the air quality massively, as they emit oxygen. This can help your general health, too. Some of the top plants which can help clean your air are:

- Areca palms
- Philodendrons
- Rubber plants
- Peace lilies
- Dracaenas

- Snake plants
- Boston ferns
- Aloe vera plants
- English ivy plants
- Spider plants

DIY INSECT DETERRENT

Keeping your plants free from bugs in the garden is tricky, and due to their high chemical content and the greenhouse gases released by the factories that make them, bug repellents are far from being eco-friendly – not to mention that they actually harm the wildlife around you. This simple hack will keep your precious plants free from creepy-crawlies but keep the planet full of them!

YOU WILL NEED:

- 2 handfuls of fresh mint leaves

- 4 garlic cloves

- 2 tbsp vinegar

- 1 litre (34 fl oz) water

- A spray bottle

Use this spray for produce plants as well as flowers and shrubs

METHOD:

1 Chuck your mint leaves and garlic in a food processor, or grind with a pestle and mortar for even more eco-friendly points.

2 Add your vinegar to a saucepan, then stir in the mint-garlic paste before adding your water. Give it a good stir, then let it cool and steep for at least 4 hours.

3 Strain your mixture and transfer it into the spray bottle, ready for use!

4 Spritz it directly onto plants you need to protect, and your bugs won't want to come near them! Can you blame them?

REGROWING YOUR OWN SALAD

Last week's waste is this week's lunch in this handy hack. Cut the bottom off your veggie of choice (just above where the root would have been) and place it in a glass of water. The glass should be snug enough that your root can stay standing without flopping over, but not tight so that it cuts off any of the plant's circulation. The whole base of the root should be submerged, but make sure some of the actual plant is still above water. Pop it on a windowsill and watch it regrow. Whenever the water looks a little yellow, replace it and give the new plant a rinse too. Within a few weeks you'll have a full and edible vegetable!

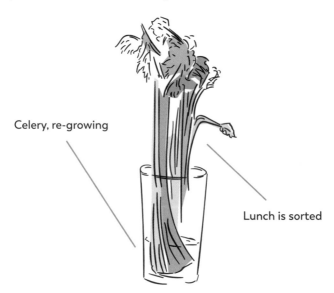

Celery, re-growing

Lunch is sorted

HERE ARE SOME VEGGIES YOU CAN USE:

- Basil

- Pak choi

- Carrots

- Celery

- Coriander

- Garlic

- Green onions

- Leeks

- Lettuce

- Rosemary

- Spring onions

- Sweet potatoes

DIY DRAINPIPE PLANTER

If you've got some old guttering going spare and an empty external wall or garden fence, this hack is for you.

YOU WILL NEED:

- Section from a gutter and end caps (the length of it doesn't matter)

- Scrap wood (same length as gutter)

- Tape measure

- Drill

- Silicone sealant

- Spray paint of any colour (if desired)

- Plank of wood (same length as gutter)

- Saw

- Spirit level

- Wood screws

- Gutter brackets

- Soil

- Plants (your choice which ones!)

METHOD:

1 Place your gutter on top of your scrap wood and measure out little markers every 10 cm (4 in.) on your gutter along the middle.

2 Carefully drill holes through each marker, using the scrap wood to protect your workspace.

3 Slot the end caps over the ends of the gutter, using your silicone sealant to secure them in place, then spray paint the outside of the gutter or leave it as it is.

4 Drill the wooden plank to your wall or fence using a spirit level to check it's straight, then attach the gutter brackets onto the plank of wood with screws.

5 Place the gutter into the brackets, then fill it with soil and your plants of choice.

BUILD YOUR OWN PALLET PATIO FURNITURE

This outdoor corner sofa requires second-hand pallets, which you can find cheap or free at marketplaces or left over at DIY shops.

FOR A SEVEN-SEATER SET, YOU WILL NEED:

- 12 pallets, 120×100 cm (47×39 in.)

- Saw

- Sandpaper

- Optional: Outdoor wood paint

- Two adjoining walls and some cushions for a backrest

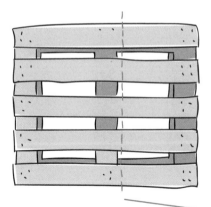

Cut down the dotted line

METHOD:

1   Lying the pallets horizontally, saw each one in half, just to the right of the central plank.

2   Stack three of the left-hand pallets on top of each other – you should have four stacks in total. The leftover pallets can be saved for other DIY projects.

3   Arrange the stacks in an L shape in the corner of your patio, up against the two walls or a wall and adjoining fence.

4   Sand the whole thing down, then if you fancy, slather on a coat or two of paint to finish!

5   When using, dig out some cushions for extra comfort.

VERTICAL INDOOR GARDENING

No garden? No problem! With this simple hack you'll be a green-fingered wunderkind in no time! There are several ways to get fun and creative with this one, but here's one suggestion to get you started.

Hang an old over-the-door shoe organizer on a fence if outdoors, or a door or wall if indoors. Poke some 3-mm (⅛-in.) holes in the bottom of each pouch and stuff the pouch with soil, then pop in your herbs or plants of choice. Give them a water when required, and you've got your very own vertical garden! (If using indoors, pop a tray underneath the organizer to catch any excess water at feeding time.)

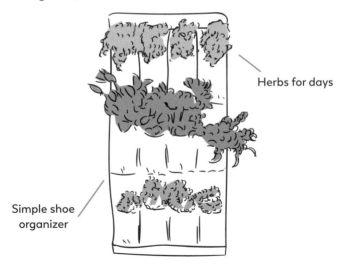

Herbs for days

Simple shoe organizer

BUILD YOUR OWN BIRD BATH

We're always happy to feed birds seeds and nuts, but they often struggle to get access to clean water. Why not give them a helping hand by creating your own bird bath for our flying friends?

You'll need either a shallow tray, a medium terracotta saucer or something else approximately 2.5 cm (1 in.) deep and 30 cm (12 in.) wide. The first step is simply to fill it with water. The second step is to add some height, and this is where you can get creative! An old stepladder, a stack of bricks or even hanging it from a regular hanging basket chain could work, but there are plenty of interesting alternatives – you could probably even find a vintage plant pot stand in a local antique shop! Pop the tray on top of your stand of choice and watch the birds flock to their new swimming pool.

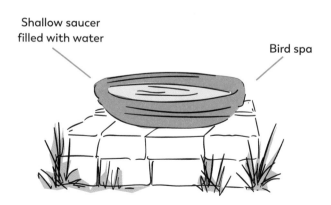

Shallow saucer filled with water

Bird spa

BUILD YOUR
OWN BEE MOTEL

Bees are key to balancing our ecosystem – we wouldn't have fruit or veg without them! However, our overuse of pesticides and air pollutants means they're dying out. Why not do your bit by cultivating a colony of bees?

Cut both ends off a large plastic bottle to make a tube. Thread a piece of string through your tube and tie a knot at the top, making sure you have extra to hang the motel off a branch. Then, stuff the tube full of hollow bamboo shoots, plant stalks and rolled up cardboard, and cut them to fit. Hang it (south-facing) from a tree in your garden at around waist height and let the bees burrow away!

**Ready for
garden visitors**

Five-star bee hotel

BUILD YOUR OWN LACEWING NEST

Lacewings are light-green bugs with wings as lacy as their name suggests, and they're brilliant at keeping aphids away – the pesky bugs that wreck your plants! This simple hack using household items will give them a fab little habitat.

Chop the bottom third off a large plastic water bottle. Roll a piece of thick, corrugated cardboard up as many times as you can and put it inside your bottle. If it slips out, tuck another strip of cardboard between your initial cardboard roll and the bottle. Then, tie a piece of string around the bottle neck and hang it somewhere sheltered roughly 2 m (79 in.) from the ground. Your lacewings will love it!

Appealing rolled-up cardboard

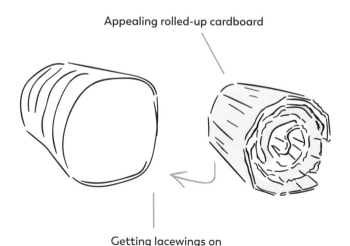

Getting lacewings on
the property ladder

BUILD YOUR
OWN LADYBIRD NEST

Ladybirds are beautiful bugs with the important job of getting rid of aphids, but did you know they hibernate throughout winter? Due to deforestation, they're often killed during hibernation, so use this simple hack to create a safe nesting spot for our dotty friends.

Arrange 12 pinecones together so they are interlocking. Pop them on a 50×50-cm (19½×19½-in.) sheet of chicken wire and lift up the corners to form a bag. Tie together with string and hang in a sheltered area of the garden – you don't want them getting washed out by the rain!

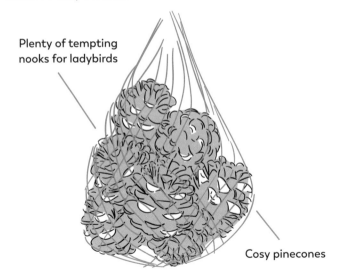

Plenty of tempting
nooks for ladybirds

Cosy pinecones

BRING ON THE BUTTERFLIES!

Butterflies aren't just pollinators; they're also indicators of a healthy ecosystem. Sadly, climate change and habitat destruction have led to a decline in the number of beautiful butterflies so we must do our bit to protect them.

The best way to attract butterflies, and therefore protect them, is to entice them with food. Place some overripe fruit on a saucer and let them come to eat – they particularly like overripe oranges. Another alternative is to make a sugar syrup using sugar and water. Whichever method you use, be sure to place your butterfly's food by some bright flowers to attract them.

Delicious overripe oranges

Butterfly fuel station

DIY IRRIGATION SYSTEM

In the same way that humans can't just drink a gallon of water at the start of the day and hope for the best, plants need watering throughout the day – especially when it's hot. Irrigation systems are designed to gradually water plants throughout the day, but they're very expensive. However, creating your own with an old plastic bottle actually works just as well!

YOU WILL NEED:

- A 2-litre (68-fl oz) plastic bottle (thoroughly cleaned or you'll attract pests) for the ground, or a 500-ml (17-fl oz) bottle for larger pots

- A bradawl

- An old sock

Simple plastic bottle

Clever plant hydration system

METHOD:

1   Using your bradawl, punch around 15 holes randomly in the lower quarter of your bottle.

2   Slot the sock over the end of the bottle to cover all of the holes – this will stop it getting clogged up by soil.

3   Plant the bottle in the soil – its neck should poke out the top.

4   Thoroughly water the soil, then fill the bottle with water. The tighter you screw the lid, the slower the release of water will be!

HARVEST YOUR OWN HERBS INDOORS

This easy-peasy make will save time, money and the planet! Having your own mini herb garden will make cooking so much simpler and minimize your waste as you won't need to keep buying packets of fresh herbs.

YOU WILL NEED:

- Seeds to grow herb plants, such as parsley, thyme, basil, oregano, coriander, rosemary, mint or chives

- A selection of jam jars

- Gravel, grit or small stones

- Compost

- Soil to cover stones

- Water

Your old pesto jar

All-you-can-eat herbs

METHOD:

1   Clean your jam jars with washing-up liquid and warm water, then rinse and leave to dry.

2   Fill 5 cm (2 in.) of your jars with gravel, grit or small stones.

3   Fill the jars about two thirds full with compost. Plant three herb seeds in each jar.

4   When shoots appear, add more soil around the base of each plant and water.

5   Place your plant on a windowsill, making sure it has the correct light levels for your chosen herb (i.e. some plants don't thrive in direct sunlight).

6   Now you can enjoy herbs all year round, and they're easy to grab when you're preparing meals.

TOP TIPS:
Helping your garden thrive

Instead of throwing eggshells in the bin, crush them up and use them as fertilizer – they contain high levels of calcium which is great for getting rid of blossom end rot.

If you've got a garden with a bit of space in it, plant some trees. It's a sure-fire way to increase wildlife traffic, especially if you're planting fruit trees. What's more, you can feast on the fruit you grow instead of buying it at the supermarket.

Soak banana skins for a couple of days in a large jar filled with water. Remove the skins (and put them in the compost bin!) then use your banana-infused water on plant roots – they'll absolutely love the nutrients!

If you're growing plants in the garden, buying plastic ties is a real waste. Cut up old T-shirts, socks or stockings to use instead – no waste required.

Want to make your garden bee-friendly? Plant some wildflowers native to your country. They're beautiful, will brighten up your garden and are super simple to maintain as they care for themselves!

Don't spend money on buying supporting canes; instead collect twigs. They look far less conspicuous and they're free!

Good quality second-hand gardening equipment can be picked up very cheaply – and sometimes even for free. Before you buy anything new, look on the Freecycle website, where you should be able to find a dedicated Freecycle community in your area. All the items are free!

Waste water from washing-up is perfect for watering gardens.

Collect fallen leaves when they are wet, then store in bin bags for two years. The result is a nutritious leaf mulch which can be used to cover your most prized plants.

COMPOSTING FOR BEGINNERS:
Fact vs fiction

Composting takes a bit of time, but if you get started today then you'll have some lovely homemade fertilizer that your future plants will adore. Here are a few myth-busters to get you started.

Composting is expensive, bins don't come cheap...
False – it's cheap and easy to start composting. Simply create a heap at the end of the garden, no bins needed.

It's not the time of year to start composting...
False – composting can be done *any* time of year.

Compost heaps can't be started on paving stones...
True – you'll need to start your heap in a partially shady area right on top of soil or grass, but make sure it's not an area prone to flooding.

There are too many rules for what can and can't go in my compost heap...

False – composting requires two types of material: greens (lawn clippings, green leaves and kitchen waste but absolutely *no* meat or dairy) and browns (straw, hay, newspaper, eggshells, coffee grounds, dried leaves and wood chips). Keep the ratio at 50:50 and you're good to go!

How to compost

Designate an area of the garden for a heap, which must be a minimum of a cubic metre. Prepare a layer of twigs and branches at the bottom of the heap to provide vertical airflow through the material; on top of this, mix in thin layers of dead flowers, manure and straw with browns and greens. Turn your compost pile every two weeks for fast results.

TRAVEL HACKS

Travel is essential and can provide us with new experiences, whether we're hopping down the motorway to work or on a plane to experience new cultures on another continent. Now that we're becoming increasingly conscious of climate change, it's time to consider how we can travel with a smaller carbon footprint.

FOOD ON THE MOVE

Tuna on the tube? Coffee in the cab? Beans on the bus? Whatever you have to munch while you're moving, limiting waste is a *must*!

Relying solely on cafes and restaurants every day isn't sustainable for the earth or the wallet. Try taking a packed lunch in a bamboo or stainless-steel container and take a reusable coffee cup for your caffeine fix. Some fancy cups and bottles even fold away into pockets! If neither of these work with your lifestyle, try taking your own portable set of cutlery and a handkerchief instead of depending on disposable forks and napkins.

Zero per cent waste

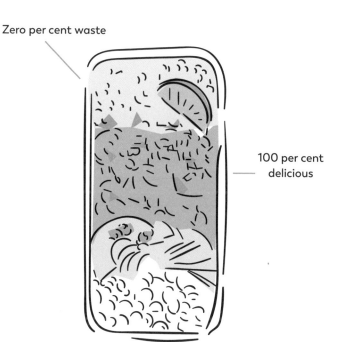

100 per cent delicious

ECO-FRIENDLY
HOTEL HACKS

Everyone wants to feel the most relaxed, Zen version of themselves while on holiday, but that doesn't mean the planet gets to relax. We tend to overindulge on holiday, so here are a couple of handy hacks to keep your hotel stay more planet-friendly.

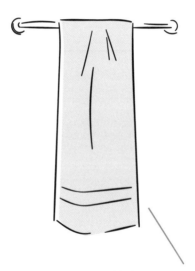

Towel belonging to an eco-warrior

Being on holiday is definitely the time to neglect the mundane, but if you wouldn't do it at home, it's probably best not to do it in a hotel.

For example, we don't tend to wash our bath towels every morning, nor do we deep clean the bedroom and change the bedding every afternoon. Most hotels have their own policy so double-check upon arrival, but usually, if you leave your towels in the bath or shower, you're asking for them to be washed. And if you hang them, you're saying "I'll reuse this!" Similarly, if you leave your "Do not disturb" sign on the door, staff won't come and clean your room and you'll be reducing the amount of cleaning chemicals, water, plastic and energy that's used.

TOP TIPS:
On the go

Composting isn't just for the home; you can keep any compostable lunch scraps in your lunchbox or in a reusable coffee cup so that you can compost it when you get back!

Check with your manager to see if it's feasible for you to work from home for a few days per week. The best way to ensure you're keeping your carbon footprint down is by simply staying at home, and you'll get the added bonus of getting to stay in your pyjamas all day.

Ditch the disposable camera. It might seem aesthetic and retro, but the reality is that they aren't very eco-friendly. If you still want to capture photos that look better than the ones you can take on your phone, buy from companies that fully refurbish old cameras. They offer the same specs as a brand new one but at a discounted price.

Try car pooling to work or school. If you live close to a colleague or school friend, see if they'd be interested in sharing lifts with you to cut down on emissions. Some workplaces even offer priority parking for car poolers, so the perks aren't just for the planet!

Don't go scrapping your car for the sake of it, but if it's on its last legs, consider getting an electric car when you're next heading to the dealership. A lot of countries are set to ban petrol and diesel cars in the near future, so you'll be doing yourself a long-term favour, too.

LEARN HOW TO ECO-DRIVE

In urban areas, good transport networks and tighter restrictions on driving have made owning a vehicle less attractive. However, sometimes there's no alternative to using your car, so try these tips to put your car into eco-drive. Did you know that underinflated tyres can cause a two per cent increase in fuel consumption? And due to an increase in weight in your car, roof racks can cause reductions in fuel economy, too. If you're driving below 40 mph (64 kmph), consider opening the window instead of turning on the air con to be more fuel-efficient and turn your engine off for stops longer than a minute to avoid wasting fuel, as we consume 5–8 per cent of fuel just by idling. While public transport is much more sustainable, eco-driving is the next best thing.

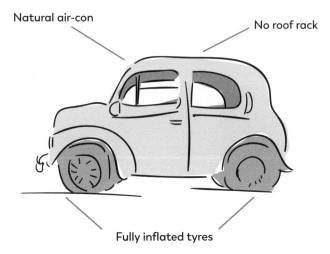

Natural air-con

No roof rack

Fully inflated tyres

SKIP TRAVEL-SIZED

It can be all too tempting to purchase mini "travel-sized" self-care products when you're travelling, but think of the waste this creates when everyone's doing it. By purchasing a cheap set of reusable travel-sized bottles (or simply reusing any old mini bottles), you can save the planet from more disposable plastic and your wallet from an unnecessary purchase. Just fill each bottle with your favourite cosmetics and you're good to go – and when you get home, use up any leftover product so the bottles can be cleaned, ready for when you next go away.

Tiny bottles

All your favourite products

CRUISE SHIPS: ECO-FRIEND OR ECO-FOE?

While slowly gliding across the sea might seem like a more planet-friendly way to see the world, research has shown polar-opposite results. In 2018, one study found that 76 out of 77 cruise ships were using heavy fuel oil, which produces the most harmful emissions to the planet – such as sulphur and nitrogen oxides – and devastates marine life. Other studies showed that, on a seven-day cruise each passenger could generate 18 days' worth of carbon, while large cruise ships can have a carbon footprint greater than 12,000 cars. So, consider skipping cruises when you're planning your next vacation.

BE SOLAR-SAVVY

A long journey in a car, or on a bus or train, equals long bouts of boredom for passengers, which is where smartphones and tablets come in. But what if the power runs out? Well, you can be eco-smart and arm yourself with solar chargers.

Stick them to the window and use the sun's rays to create energy for your boredom-busting gadgets. You'll be able to keep yourself, or your passengers, screen-ready with a free conscience for the whole journey.

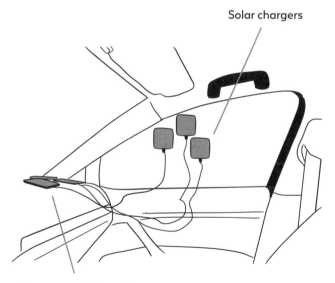

Solar chargers

Phones – only leave them on the dashboard when the car is stationary

TOP TIPS:
Planet-friendly flying

The emissions from aviation are a major contributor to global warming, so the best way to minimize your carbon footprint is simply not to fly, although that's not always practical. Here are some tips for flying that won't cost the earth.

Find out which airlines have smaller carbon footprints and fly with them.

Some search engines offset the emissions from your flight by planting trees or installing solar panels in developing countries, so by booking through them, you're minimizing your environmental impact.

Flying economy won't just help your wallet, it'll help you minimize your carbon footprint. In business and first class, not only is more space taken up (meaning more planes are in the air to accommodate our luxurious lifestyles) but there's the single-waste luxuries (plastic bottles of champagne, eye masks and blankets), the TV screens and air con (which drastically increase fuel consumption) and individual beds, not to mention the carbon footprint of the airport lounges that all make the journey a lot more unsustainable.

Don't pack too much; if everyone took less luggage, the plane wouldn't use quite as much fuel.

If you're flying further afield, avoid multiple stopovers. Planes use the most fuel while taking off and landing, so the more runway time you can avoid, the better. Fly from your nearest airport and use public transport to get there to minimize the emissions of driving.

Flying is far from being sustainable, but there are certainly ways to make it more eco-friendly!

TOURIST TRAPS: "WILD" LIFE

When abroad, be wary of animal-based attractions. Elephants and camels weren't designed to carry a weight as heavy as us humans, and sloths don't enjoy cuddling our necks for selfies. While there are plenty of sanctuaries around the world doing their best to care for animals, there are some that aren't as innocent as they may seem. Here are some tips to help you check if an animal attraction is ethical or not.

THINGS TO WATCH OUT FOR:

- Do the animals seem happy? If they're in a really small enclosure and appear to be pacing with their heads hung, they're probably not living their best lives. A happy animal will be acting as they would in the wild, with plenty of space to explore.

- Are they being well fed? Some animals are supposed to have visible ribs, but the amount of blubber on an animal is often a good indicator as to whether they're being fed properly. Seals and penguins can often be overfed (as feeding time is a lucrative attraction), whereas horses and camels are often given limited food, as the more time they spend eating the less time they can spend giving customers rides. A happy animal will graze during the day, and won't seem absolutely astounded at the sight of food at dinner time.

- Are they covered in scars? Do the workers seem to use force to get the animals to follow orders? Do they use hooks? These are all signs that their owners might be mistreating them.

- Some sanctuaries welcome the assistance of tourists in caring for animals, helping clear their enclosures, feeding and cleaning them, but before handing over any money, make sure you've done thorough research into the charity so you can ensure you're supporting rehabilitation, not exploitation.

SIGNS OF AN ETHICAL WILDLIFE EXPERIENCE:

- Experiences that put conservation and education at the heart of what they do, rather than photo opportunities.

- Locally based operators who care about the community and the surrounding environment.

- Tours or experiences that take part in small groups.

- Tour guides or staff who are knowledgeable about the wildlife and the local environment.

- Clear policies on acceptable and unacceptable behaviour around the wildlife.

LOCATION, LOCATION, LOCATION

One of the first things you should consider when choosing to travel is *why* you're going; careful thinking leads to conscious travelling!

DO YOU WANT TO SEE THE SIGHTS?

Why not try taking a coach there? You'll get to see all the exciting sights from the window and be right in the middle of this new wave of culture, instead of being suspended in the sky!

DO YOU WANT TO MAKE A CHANGE?

If helping other people makes you tick, pick a country that really needs aid. Visit a country which is struggling following a natural disaster, for example. You could take hygiene products, food, clothes and even toys for the less fortunate children.

DO YOU JUST NEED A BREAK?

If you're in need of a break, could a staycation function just as well as a flight abroad? Staycations require less energy and money, and staying in the country you live in would be less stressful, given that you speak the language and know how the local transport system works.

SLOW TRAVEL

Modern-day travelling has become faster and faster – and it's now perfectly normal to be able to visit foreign cities, hundreds of miles away from our own countries, for the space of a single weekend. Our experience on these trips is often condensed into seeing the main sights and grabbing the Instagram-worthy photo before we must rush to return home. However, this travel mind-set is having an adverse effect on communities – who find it hard to sustain intense levels of tourism – and the environment, as we take more plane journeys.

One way to embrace the joys of travelling without the harmful impact is with slow travel. Slow travel is about replacing plane journeys with other modes of overland transport, such as trains or buses, and it can even involve walking or cycling part of your route as well. Not only does this reduce your carbon footprint, but it encourages you to travel differently, allowing you to more fully connect with the people, cultures and environments that you visit.

KEEP ON CAMPING

Planning a camping trip? Try these earth-friendly tips to minimize waste and make sure you keep on your campsite neighbours' good side!

- There's naturally a temptation to take single-use items when camping to reduce washing-up, but you can limit your eco-impact by planning meals ahead and taking your own food.

- Batch cook your snacks and take them in one box, as this avoids lots of single-use plastic. Check out the recipe for fab vegan s'mores bars on page 160!

- Don't bother buying water bottles – take your own and fill them up at the campsite or at local restaurants and bars and, instead of taking disposable cutlery and crockery, take reusable items and some washing-up equipment.

- Use eco-friendly washing up liquid so as not to harm the local environment. You can make this ahead of your trip: simply pour 3 tbsp of liquid Castile soap, 0.25 l (0.4 pt) warm water, 2 tbsp white vinegar and a few drops of essential oil into a bottle (screw-cap or a squeezy top is fine). Close the lid firmly, give it a good shake to mix and then use as normal.

- Plastic is undoubtedly one of the best materials you can use to keep dry when you're up against the elements. However, you can limit how much other plastic you're using by taking airtight containers or beeswax wraps instead of cling film – after all, when staying so close to wildlife, the least we could do is make sure we don't ruin the habitat with careless plastic waste!

- Make sure you leave your campsite as spotless as it was when you left. Don't leave any litter – not just because it's unfair to the next campers, but because it's unfair to the wildlife. Fill in any holes you've dug with soil, and make sure any cigarette stubs are binned as they hamper growth of new plants!

PLANT-BASED "HAPPY CAMPER" BARS

Give this plant-based granola bar recipe a go for the perfect, waste-free camping treat!

YOU WILL NEED:

- 6 dates, roughly chopped

- 120 ml (4 fl oz) water

- 60 ml (2 fl oz) maple syrup

- 2 tbsp chia seeds

- ¼ tsp salt

- 220 g (8 oz) oats

- 250 g (9 oz) crushed vegan biscuits

- A handful of vegan mini marshmallows

- 40 g (1.5 oz) dark chocolate, chopped

- 1 tsp dairy-free butter

METHOD:

1   Preheat your oven to 180°C (350°F). Pop your dates, water, syrup, chia seeds and salt in a blender – don't turn it on yet! Leave to stand for about 5 minutes, then blend away until smooth-ish.

2   Toast the oats in a dry pan over a medium–high heat, stirring frequently. Once done, put these into a mixing bowl.

3   Add the oats, crackers, marshmallows, chocolate and your sticky date mixture, and mix well until all of the dry ingredients are covered.

4   Grease a loaf tin using dairy-free butter, then pour your mixture in, ensuring it's spread evenly. Press down to make it compact and bake for 20 minutes.

5   Remove from the oven, let it cool and cut into bars. Try not to eat these all at once, and save a few for your campmates! Or don't...

DIY SUSTAINABILITY PLANNER

Whenever you plan a trip somewhere, whether it's a one-day excursion or week-long holiday, try making a sustainability planner to keep track of your environmental impact. If you use your planner for every trip you make, it'll help you visualize what kind of impact your travelling has on the planet and could help you make smart choices about holidays, no matter how big or small!

Your pages (preferably digital!) might look something like this:

EXCURSIONS

Excursions	Location	Who/what could I be impacting?	How can I minimize impact?
Hike	Glacier National Park	Other hikers	Minimize waste
		Residents	Keep noise down
Swimming and picnic	Lake McDonald	Wildlife	Leave no trace and respect their habitat
		Other swimmers	Stick to an area and tidy up

TRANSPORT

Transport	Location	Carbon dioxide emissions	How can I minimize impact?
Plane	To: Montana	High	No stopover
Train	To: Hostel	Medium	Economy
Bike	To: Lake	None	Push bike, not e-bike
Walk	To: National Park	None	Minimize waste

GET BUSY
WITH BEESWAX

If you're keen on the environment as well as staying dry while out walking, this one is for you. Waterproofing your gear is an essential precaution for any trek; however, most spray-on proofers are made up of various synthetic chemicals. If you're keen on avoiding these, here's a natural alternative.

Beeswax is featured in many proofing products anyway, but used in its pure form, it's doing a similar job without having been heavily processed. It can be rubbed directly onto garments, bags and shoes – just expect them to be a little waxy and pleasantly fragrant as a result.

PERFECT PACKING HACKS

If you're being super eco-friendly you might only be taking carry-on, so here are some handy hacks for packing efficiently.

STUFF IT IN YOUR SHOE

Shoes take up a lot of space no matter what, so you might as well make the most of them. Put your cosmetics in one sock, put that sock in its matching counterpart and then stuff them in your shoes! Make sure the lids are firmly on, though – you don't want to be stuck with a wet, greasy shoe for a week.

ROLL IT UP

For each of your items with thinner fabric (such as T-shirts or swimsuits), try laying them flat in front of you, folding them lengthways into thirds and rolling into thin rolls. This doesn't work for chunkier fabric (jeans and jumpers) but is perfect for organizing smaller pieces.

WEAR THE WEIGHTY ONES

Okay, so this one might be cheating a bit, but if you really can't fit something in but it's an absolute necessity, wear it while you're travelling! Thick coats or big boots can all be worn (and removed) in transit if required.

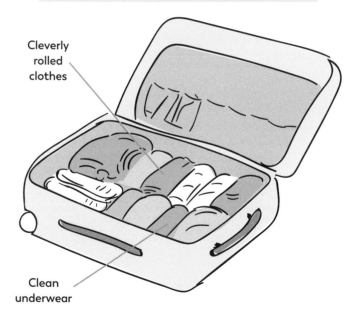

Cleverly rolled clothes

Clean underwear

PLANET-FRIENDLY PLACES TO STAY

Being eco-conscious on your travels doesn't stop at where you go, how you get there and what you do. Try these tips to find some hidden holiday gems.

HOSTELS

Okay, they might not always be the flashiest or most "Instagrammable" places to stay, but hostels are a great way of keeping both monetary and environmental costs low. Sharing bedrooms, bathrooms and kitchens minimizes carbon dioxide emissions and water wastage, and you might make a best friend for life!

BED AND BREAKFASTS

Some sites allow you to live in other peoples' houses and rent out a room (or sometimes an entire house) for a little while. It's a great and affordable way to stay, a sort of hybrid between a hostel and a private house. Because there's no requirement for "state-of-the-art" amenities as in fancy hotels, these tend to be fairly eco-friendly, too.

CAMPING

We've already touched on this one, but a great way to ensure you're minimizing your carbon footprint wherever you stay is to simply take your own hotel with you! Find a plot of land (with permission from the landowner) and set up your own little tent. Enjoy life the simple way, without wasting water and by living off what the land provides.

CONCLUSION

There are so many tiny changes you can make to your daily routine that you might not even realize make a difference, but they really do. With any luck, you can now use a needle, thread and a spot of recycled fabric to replicate more sustainable versions of just about anything!

The best way to keep living consciously is to use what the earth gives us, and to stop depending on artificial alternatives. If we take from nature, the best we can do is at least *try* to return the favour – similar to how carbon-offsetting flights work.

Whether you're making changes in the bathroom, the kitchen or when you're cleaning, hopefully this book has given you a few planet-friendly hacks which you can live by for years to come.

Good luck on your journey to sustainability; it might not always be the simplest, but it's definitely worth it!

NOTES

IMAGE CREDITS

THE RESPONSIBLE
TRAVELLER

Karen Edwards

Paperback

978-1-80007-388-3

Here is your ticket to positive, guilt-free, sustainable and ethical travel. *The Responsible Traveller* will show you how to make real changes that result in more thoughtful and conscientious travels, while also doing your very best for Planet Earth. Learn about the environmental and social effects of tourism and increase your cultural awareness.

THE PLANET-FRIENDLY KITCHEN

Karen Edwards

Hardback

978-1-78783-691-4

We all have the power to make a difference. The *Planet-Friendly Kitchen* sets out the facts about sustainable food in a clear and straightforward way, with tips and advice to help you make informed choices about the way you shop, the food you buy, and the way you cook them. Contains over 30 delicious, environmentally conscious recipes.

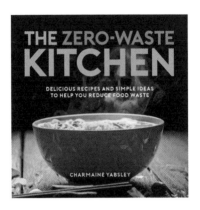

THE ZERO-WASTE KITCHEN

Charmaine Yabsley

Hardback

978-1-78783-690-7

The Zero-Waste Kitchen is your essential guide to shopping smarter and making meals that go the extra mile, and includes:

- An A–Z guide to common leftovers and how they can be used
- Easy-to-follow recipes for using up ingredients that go to waste
- And much, much more!

SAVE THE WORLD

Louise Bradford

Paperback

978-1-78783-034-9

There is little doubt that our beautiful planet is now under huge threat. We need to take action before it's too late, and we can all do our bit to help. This guide is full of simple tips we can all incorporate into our daily lives, and will demonstrate how small eco-friendly changes can have a huge positive effect on the world around us.

Have you enjoyed this book?
If so, find us on Facebook at
Summersdale Publishers,
on Twitter at @Summersdale and
on Instagram at @summersdalebooks
and get in touch. We'd love to hear from you!

www.summersdale.com